"Words and phrases from various Native American languages liberally stud the well-cadenced text, enhancing the already authentic atmosphere."
                                        —*Publishers Weekly*

"The tales are easy to follow and to envision, but they can be understood and interpreted on many levels. Striking black-and-white illustrations."
                                        —*Booklist*

Flying with the Eagle, Racing the Great Bear

Stories From Native North America
Told by Joseph Bruchac

Troll Medallion

For all of our sons — J.B.

This edition published in 2001.

Library of Congress Cataloging-in-Publication Data

Bruchac, Joseph, (date)
Flying with the eagle, racing the great bear: stories from Native
North America / told by Joseph Bruchac.
p.   cm.
Includes bibliographical references.
Summary: A collection of traditional tales which present the
heritage of various Indian nations, including the Wampanoag,
Cherokee, Osage, Lakota, and Tlingit.
ISBN 0-8167-3026-1 (lib.)   ISBN 0-8167-3027-X (pbk.)
1. Indians of North America—Legends.   2. Indians of North
America—Rites and ceremonies—Juvenile literature.
[1. Indians of North America—Legends.]   I. Title.
E98.F6B893   1993   [398.2 '08997]—dc20   93-21966

Text copyright © 1993 by Joseph Bruchac.
Illustrations copyright © 1993 by Murv Jacob.

Published by Troll Medallion, an imprint and registered
trademark of Troll Communications L.L.C.

First published in hardcover by BridgeWater Books.

Printed in the United States of America.

10   9   8   7   6   5   4

CONTENTS

FLYING WITH THE EAGLE,

RACING THE GREAT BEAR

INTRODUCTION

There comes a time in every boy's life when he must step into manhood, a time when a boy must leave his home, leave the protection of his mother and father, and go out to prove to himself that he can survive and grow. That fact seems to have been recognized by every human culture. Clearly defined rituals, or rites of passage, were developed to help the young man make that change and better understand the responsibilities of his new adult roles.

Among the more than four hundred different tribal nations that existed in North America before the coming of the Europeans, there were many different rites of passage for young men. The many varieties of the sweat lodge, the practices of fasting in isolation and praying for a guiding vision, and the deeply symbolic ceremonies in which the older men took on the guise of ancestral beings and powerful spirits are among the better-known rites of passage practiced by many Native nations.

One powerful way in which the meanings of this transition have been taught for thousands of years is through traditional stories. Two decades ago, when I first began telling the traditional stories that were part of my own Native heritage, it was to share them with my own children. They were small boys then, but as they grew and changed, my understanding of how the stories worked grew with them.

Many of the stories I've been given are tales designed not only to help the boy find his way to full manhood but also to help the man remember the boy within himself, so that he can be sympathetic and helpful to the coming generations. The old tales grow with us. Now my sons, Jim and Jesse, are young men, telling the stories they learned to the children they teach. That is how the circle of stories works, linking the generations.

Like all the Native American stories I know, the ones in this book are designed both to entertain and to educate. I offer them as a few examples of the ways in which the many different tribal nations of North America recognized the need to guide and gently channel young men as they grew.

I have divided the book into four sections because four is a number of powerful and magical importance to Native peoples: There are four seasons, four winds, four directions, four stages in a person's life. It is interesting in these tales how often each young man faces trials in clusters of four.

One of the reasons I have devoted so much of my own life to the understanding and the respectful telling of traditional Native stories is my strong belief that now, more than ever, these tales have much to teach us— whether we are of Native ancestry or not. We learn about ourselves by understanding others. Our own traditions can be made stronger only when we pay attention to and respect the traditions of people who are different from ourselves. Hearing or reading the stories of the Native peoples of North America will not make any of us Native Americans, but it may help make all of us more human.

THE NORTHEAST

One of the most common rites of passage found throughout most of Native North America is the vision quest. It is known among the Lakota of the western plains as hanblecheyapi, which translates into English as "crying for a vision."

This practice, however, is not limited to the Native American people of the West. As we see in the Anishinabe story "The Dream Fast," it is also present among the peoples of the northeastern woodlands. Many Native people still believe that special guidance is available from the forces of nature and that by fasting and praying in an isolated place, the spiritual senses are sharpened. Animals may come and offer themselves as guides, and a boy may, indeed, find himself flying with the eagle—as we see later on in the book.

The experience a boy has on his first vision quest often shapes the rest of his life. There are many different ways of seeking a vision, but most of them involve going to a place removed from other human beings and

remaining there without food for as long as several days.

The ordeal is also a part of the experience. Going out without the protection of parents, symbolically orphaned as in the story of "White Weasel," is a common theme in these tales. When a boy does this, he may encounter dangerous, even malevolent, forces. The stories tell us he may overcome adversity by making use of the good teachings given him by his elders.

Such recurring themes mirror or sharpen the experiences expected in "real life." Sooner or later, each of us must be like Swift Runner in the Iroquois story "Racing the Great Bear" and challenge our own monsters, with our survival in the balance. These stories tell us that if we have listened well to our elders, we can rely upon ourselves when the need arises.

Finally, "Granny Squannit and the Bad Young Man" remains one of my favorite tales in this section. It is not only a rite-of-passage story but also a good example of the way Native children are disciplined. Beating children or even shouting loudly at them is avoided by Native American parents. Instead, telling lesson stories and speaking calmly and clearly to children to try to lead them in the right direction are common practices. As a last resort, a parent might threaten an unruly child with monsters that prey only upon disobedient children.

Native youngsters are encouraged to refer to elders, whether they are human, animal, or a force of nature, as "Grandmother" or "Grandfather." As a combination of elder and fearful being, Granny Squannit is called upon to help teach a particularly bad boy the proper way to behave.

Part Two:
Beyond The Myths

To this point our book has focused on the four most pervasive myths of adoption:

1. The birthmother obviously doesn't care about her child or she wouldn't have given him away.

2. Secrecy in every phase of the adoption process is necessary to protect all parties.

3. Both the birthmother and birthfather will forget about their unwanted child.

4. If the adoptee really loved his adoptive family, he would not have to search for his birthparents.

These statements represent the prevalent myths in today's adoption drama. We began our book with these myths in order to firmly set in our reader's mind the present image of adoption. Sadly, the four myths are accepted to some extent by everyone. Effects of the myths go beyond outdated agency policies as they permeate interactions between each adult and child touched by adoption.

The following chapters are aimed at making adoption today as myth-free as possible. As we introduce concepts of adoption counseling, pregnancy counseling, and open communication, readers must evaluate how they feel about our practices. If you feel uneasy about a particular idea, check which myth you still (perhaps unconsciously) believe. Our concepts are tested daily—even hour by hour—in human exchanges and interactions we will share. If we are all fortunate, adoption will grow beyond the myths.

5
The Vulnerability
of Adoptive Parents

*"My infertility resides in my heart as
an old friend. I do not hear from it
for weeks at a time, and then, a
moment, a thought, a baby
announcement or some such thing,
and I will feel the tug—maybe even
be sad or shed a few tears. And I
think, 'There's my old friend.' It will
always be part of me. . . ."*
Barbara Eck Menning
*Infertility: A Guide for the
Childless Couple (1977)*

Typically the "American Dream" consists of the following
ingredients: growing up, obtaining a usable education that
leads to a comfortable job, getting married, and easily
producing children. An alternate ingredient of adopting children is not contemplated since the ability to bear children
is always viewed as a "given." In this chapter, we deal with
people and their feelings when denied this given. We will
introduce the reader to the special type of pain the infertility
experience awakens, then explore how a couple's infertility
crisis shapes their initial approach to an adopted child.

Finally we will focus on the reality of the adoptive family structure and the struggle to accept that reality.

A STRUGGLE TO ACCEPT INFERTILITY

We are indoctrinated early in life to dream of someday having
children like ourselves. Most couples assume this will automatically happen when they are ready to have children. A
couple's first reaction to the shock of not conceiving is to try
harder. This, in turn, begins a period where the need to get
pregnant seems to overshadow everything else. Many couples tell us of the frustration and tension that develop in their
sexual relationship. They feel required to perform at a
specific, clinically determined, time. Love and spontaneity are
removed from their sexual relationship. Instead, everything
is focused on their one goal in life—to achieve a pregnancy.

Sadness and defeat grow as the couple struggles with
the often long and painful interval of infertility tests, unsuccessful medical and surgical treatments, and possibly mis-
carriages. Our experience has been that the crisis of infertility
impacts women more profoundly than their spouses. This is
partially explained by the inability of the woman to
experience the physical changes of pregnancy. Frequently,
women relate to us tearful episodes upon learning of a
friend's pregnancy. Gloria was so obsessed with her own inability to conceive that she was even unable to visit her best
friend when that friend gave birth to her first child. Gloria
could not face the reality of anyone else having a baby—the
baby she was being denied.

Other couples caught by the agony of infertility imagine
what it would be like to have a baby. They picture the Lamaze
classes, being in the delivery room, the joy of seeing their
baby born, and the look on their own father's face when he
first sees his grandson or granddaughter. Fantasies such as
these are common because they allow a temporary escape
for the couple desperate to undo the nightmare of their
childlessness.

Society unknowingly adds to the struggle by depicting
in articles and television commercials what is "right" for a

person of a certain age and marital status. Friends and family members ask innocent yet painful questions that presuppose the couple's ability to have babies. Parents are famous for regularly asking about when they will become grandparents. Their questions pointedly assume that the couple is "selfishly" choosing to deprive them of a grandchild. As a result, outside pressure to get pregnant is intense and the final reality of infertility often dramatic or disastrous.

Janice refused to believe her doctor's statement that if her surgery was successful she would become pregnant within six months. Instead, she continued beyond that time keeping her temperature chart, having sex at the specified time, and in the specific position. Finally, when passing a bookstore featuring a book on the joys of pregnancy, Janice stopped and the years of frustration took over. Janice cried right there, in the bookstore. "I did not care what anybody thought. I had waited a long time for that cry."

Betty recalls, after years of repeatedly unsuccessful surgeries, "The pressure had become so great that I offered my husband a divorce. I felt defective and unclean." Sadly, we hear many similar versions of Betty's story from both husbands and wives. It seems vulnerable spouses who view themselves as defective often feel compelled to free their mate by offering them a divorce.

For others the finality of an empty nursery and childlessness releases feelings of failure and hopelessness that take on dramatic proportions. "One night I felt I simply could not face another day," writes Kaye Halverson. "Pills, poisons, and car accidents kept flashing through my mind, and then the peace of death and joy of heaven."* Kaye subsequently worked through her crisis partly with the help of a national infertility support group—RESOLVE. This organization was started by infertile couples to offer counseling, referral, and support to others struggling to understand and accept infertility.

---

*Halverson, Kaye, with Karen M. Hess, *The Wedded Unmother,* Minneapolis, MN. Augsburg Publishing House, 1980.

APPROACHING ADOPTION

Not every couple resolves their infertility by seeking to adopt, nor should couples automatically believe adoption is their best or only alternative. Our work, of course, revolves primarily around adoption. Therefore, in this chapter we focus on couples who have opted for adoption rather than a child-free life. The following case history illustrates one such couple's initial approach to adoption and their subsequent evolution.

Ed and Marisa, ages 33 and 30, approached an adoption agency after seven years of marriage. They had been attempting unsuccessfully to have a child biologically for over three years. They initially had postponed starting a family so that Ed could finish his Ph.D. degree and secure a university teaching position. Marisa was also busy with her own career. When they finally decided to have a baby, they assumed Marisa would get pregnant immediately. When she didn't, they began the extensive and frustrating procedure of infertility testing. It seemed like an endless process, with month after month of disappointment. Marisa cried each month when her period started. She also found herself becoming easily depressed when friends became pregnant, and she began to question herself as a woman.

Both Ed and Marisa commented on the fact that up to this point in their lives they had been able to achieve anything they wanted, but now they felt powerless to achieve what they wanted most. When the doctor finally finished testing and found no reason for their infertility, he suggested adoption.

Initially Ed and Marisa were not sure they wanted to adopt. They wanted a child of their "own." As they discussed it repeatedly they realized that raising a child was more important to them than whether or not they gave birth. They decided to explore adoption. It was a little frightening, though, to make that first phone call. They were apprehensive about the mysterious agency and wondered if they had to be "perfect" in order to be accepted. After calling several agencies they learned that there is a nationwide shortage of Caucasian infants, compared to the large number of couples wanting to adopt. This made them feel even more nervous about measuring up to the obviously rigorous selection process.

When they finally reached the stage of an adoption home study, Ed and Marisa had feelings of ambivalence, nervousness, and hostility toward the agency—hostility at having to depend on strangers in order to have "their" child. They still felt the need to appear perfect to win the agency's approval. If Marisa and Ed had chosen independent adoption, they would not have had to deal with these negative feelings toward the agency as the "decision maker."

As they began to know their social worker, they were able to relax some. With her assistance, they began to learn about the realities of adoption. They found themselves discussing adoption at home every day. They explored such emotionally charged issues as how they would feel about the birthparents, when and how they would start discussing adoption with their child, and what level of openness they would risk. They realized that before entering the adoption process, they had never thought about birthparents and their feelings. All their thoughts had been solely directed toward the baby.

They also talked to friends and relatives about adoptive issues. In discussing and thinking about adoption, they discovered that in spite of their fears and anger toward the agency's involvement in achieving parenthood, they had grown in the process. They felt better prepared to be parents, especially adoptive parents. Adoption seemed an acceptable way of forming a family. Now they knew that an adopted child would be their "own."

When the social worker told them they were approved for adoption, they were thrilled and relieved—the process of "proving themselves" was over (again, this element would not have been necessary if they had chosen independent adoption). They could simply look forward to the baby's arrival. This waiting period, however, also proved difficult. Marisa found herself waiting daily for the phone to ring. They soon began to wonder if they would ever get their call. Once more they were reminded that their destiny was out of their control.

Finally, their day arrived and they excitedly drove to the agency to meet their new daughter. Again, they had some anxieties. They wondered if they would be good parents, if they would love Kimberly right away, and how they would feel if she were ugly. When they were presented a seven-day-old baby girl with a full head of black hair, dark eyes, and fair skin, they both melted. This was the happiest moment of their married lives. They were filled with awe, excitement, and anticipation for their future.

Six months later during their social worker's last home visit, Ed and Marisa proudly showed off their daughter Kimberly and related all of her accomplishments. They felt sure she was the brightest, most beautiful baby ever! Both recalled that they hadn't experienced feelings of love instantly—in the beginning it sort of felt like they were babysitting someone else's child. But as they cared for her day by day the feelings of love grew.

Once they had fully bonded with their new daughter, Ed and Marisa had some difficulty in remembering Kimberly's birthparents. They knew that these possessive feelings were natural because the baby was very much theirs, and it took a conscious effort to think of Kimberly's second set of parents. Ed and Marisa recalled that when they first discussed adoption, they had never thought about the individuals who would bear their child. They certainly had no appreciation of their feelings or their rights. It was as if they never existed. Yet, after the adoption education process and after exposure to numerous birthparents, they had grown to both understand and care for these two people. They reported that they were not threatened by Kimberly's birthparents. In fact, Ed and Marisa requested as much data and information about them as possible to ultimately share with their daughter. Ed and Marisa treasured the letters, pictures, and gifts they received, because, "these items will be very special to Kimberly in later years." They both felt very comfortable and natural in writing to Kimberly's birthmother. "After all," they noted, "she has given us so much!"

Ed and Marisa's story is representative of couples seeking to become adoptive parents. Our experience with these couples has taught us that three distinct phases exist and must be addressed. Infertility resolution is one such critical phase. Resolving the childbearing loss dramatically parallels the same stages of grief as experienced when a family member dies (denial, anger, sadness, and finally acceptance). Regrettably, assistance in this area is often overlooked or summarily dealt with in most adoption programs.

We see as a second phase the adoption education process—either an educational program through an independent adoption organization or through an adoption agency. For most adoptive parents this is an emotionally charged period because some other individual (either a social worker in the case of agency adoption or the birthmother in the case of independent adoption) has control of their fate. You will remember that Ed and Marisa experienced some natural anger at having to appear perfect to win agency approval.

The final phase involves the couple exploring the realities of adoptive parenthood. These realities focus on the adoptive family structure—its similarities to and differences from biological parenthood. As with Ed and Marisa, couples in this phase integrate their role without displacing the birthparents' place in the adoptee's life.

We will address in detail each of these three phases. Overall, the dynamics of what the couple faces can be best understood when viewed from the aspect of their lack of control or autonomy throughout their adoption experience. The first experience with loss of control (their infertility) is potentially the most draining. Being denied a natural child by infertility can be crippling unless the couple grows to accept this child's loss—this is both the first phase and the first struggle to become adoptive parents.

Couples vary in just how far they have progressed in accepting infertility when they first approach the adoption intermediary. Some are committed to adoption as their alternative to a child-free life. These couples may have even completed the process of mourning their never-to-be-born child. For these couples, an adoptive child is not a replacement but a child wanted for himself. Keith, a thirty-six-year-old adoptive father, explained this to the birthmother of his son in the following excerpt from his letter to her:

Because my wife and I value our marriage, we have both taken the time and effort to make our marriage a happy and giving relationship. One of the hardest periods of our marriage was when we desired to have children, but found out that we couldn't. It was extremely frustrating to see our friends and other people with their babies, and then realize that we couldn't have our own family. At first this was hard to accept. However, as soon as we realized that we were not able to have our own child, we immediately began inquiring into adoption and taking the necessary steps to adopt. The fact that my wife is adopted, together with the excellent and close relationship which she enjoys with her adoptive parents, made adoption very easy to accept. We did not consider adoption a last alternative, but instead merely a way of obtaining a baby that we wanted to have very much.

As his letter reflects, Keith and his wife decided not to lead a child-free life only after they had dealt with and accepted the fact their marriage would not produce that child. Their decision to adopt was motivated by a desire to experience parenthood.

By contrast, numerous couples begin the adoption process without first facing and dealing with the finality of their infertility. Although not one of our primary myths, a fiction widely believed by these couples and by their parents and friends is that "once you adopt, you will relax and have a child of your own." Therefore, rather than acknowledge their infertility, these couples pursue adoption in order to later obtain their desired pregnancy. Adoption is thus viewed as a temporary measure in their desperate quest for their "own" baby.

Wherever the couple may be in resolving their infertility, every couple approaching adoption benefits from the assistance of a professional adoption counselor. The adoption counselor must understand the vulnerability of these prospective parents, yet not overprotect them by avoiding painful topics. Couples need to accept the loss of their unborn child before they begin a relationship with the adoptee.

Resolution of infertility does not mean they will ever forget that they could not bear their "own child," but it does mean they can see their adopted child for the individual he will become. They can also accept themselves without lingering feelings of failure, remorse, or anger. They can acknowledge the realities of adoptive parenthood without thinking they are second best to natural parents. To accomplish this, the couple must discuss openly their infertility experience, their grief, and their reasons for forming a family through adoption.

Adoption is not, of course, the only alternative for the infertile couple. If they do seek adoption, however, the adoptee must be wanted not as a "substitute" but as an individual who needs two parents to nurture, guide, and love him.

The second phase in assuming the role of adoptive parents involves the counseling and educational services provided by the professional adoption intermediary. Here, too, the empathy and wisdom of a trained intermediary is essential. In the case of agency adoption, the couple believes their primary task is to convince an adoption social worker that they are stable, secure, and "together" people. Such a selling job allows the couple little time to explore the fears of adoptive parenthood such as, "Can we love someone else's child?" and "Will our parents accept an adopted grandchild?" or "What will our friends think?"

The couple might even find themselves unable to discuss with their social worker any deep-seated fears they may have of becoming parents. Even final acceptance by an adoption agency does not end a couple's struggle or return control to them. Acceptance by the agency just begins a second long and often painful period of waiting. Although pregnancy also involves a waiting period, the two experiences are not similar. A husband and wife "expecting" a baby know their due date, and the time before the birth is accompanied by outward physical changes in the couple and society's approval. A husband and wife "awaiting" an adoptive placement do not know when their baby is due (or even how old that baby will be).

In independent adoption, the adoptive couple still has no due date, but they do not have to "prove themselves" to an agency social worker. This enables them to feel more in control of their own lives and their own adoption. Instead of assuming a passive role and waiting for the agency to call them, they are taking an active role, writing their "birthmother letter" and then distributing their letters through personal networking efforts in the hopes of locating a birthmother.

Society, in addition, does not assist the adoptive couple in preparing for their role change to parenthood. Even family members and friends may not provide approving support to the adopting couple. This can be partly explained because the couple shows no outward signs that they will soon be parents. More significant, however, is the general lack of understanding about adoption. Since most of those around us tenaciously believe the four myths of adoption, individual reactions to a couple's decisions to adopt will vary. There are those around the adopting couple who anxiously verbalize a fear that the "birthmother will reclaim her child." Others are over-solicitous in their support, "Gee, you are really special to adopt someone else's child. I don't think I could." Finally, some are unknowingly cruel, "You're so lucky—adopting is the easy way of having a child." All these comments and subtle messages motivate the couple to regain control of their life—free from scrutiny—once the baby is actually placed in their arms.

When placement day finally arrives, we hear many couples talk of their compulsion "to get my baby out of this agency (or hospital) and home." Their urgent need is to escape to the sanction and privacy of their home, "dress him in his own clothes," and thus regain control of their life and family. Pain from the loss of any biological child and the frustration of outside scrutiny has extended over a long period.

Once adoptive parents do have their long awaited child in their home, they are tempted to pretend or forget he was adopted. Nanette, an adoptive mother, describes it best in this way:

Intellectually, I know that the baby was adopted, but emotionally I can pretend that he has been and is totally mine in every way.

Pretending as if the adoptive child was born naturally to the couple is common and takes many forms. Frequently, the couples working with us speak of a type of complete (yet innocent appearing) denial, "I keep forgetting he was adopted." Other couples describe their "as if" attitude as follows, "I have always considered Andrew adopted, but I have never really seen myself as an adoptive mother."

No matter the form, adoptive parents living this pretense are seeking to be normal parents. Seeking to be normal really means denying that they first had to go through the infertility nightmare and then suffer through the adoption process. Another part of the need for this "as if" pretense is a desire for societal and familial acceptance and approval. Because myths create misconceptions and apprehensions among family members, friends, and the neighborhood grocery clerk, the adoptive couple soon learns it is easier not to mention adoption. A frequent comment among adoptive parents is, "I get tired of answering questions— insensitive questions that often hurt."

The final contributor to a couple's need to pretend is the largely unconscious feeling that the child's birthparents are his "real mother and father." Considering the work it took to become parents, some adoptive couples fear the day their child might decide to search for his "true" parents (fourth myth). Overall, this pretense results in more feelings of helplessness, sadness, and defeat.

THE REALITIES OF ADOPTIVE PARENTHOOD

We see the final phase of becoming an adoptive parent as accepting the realities of this form of parenthood. In effect, this means progressing from pretending that the child was born naturally to the couple to the pain-free integration of the realities of adoption. Here our approach revolves around sensitizing adoptive parents to three often blunt concepts:

1. **Adoption is a lifetime experience.** (It does not go away when the intermediary contact is over.)

2. **Adoptive parents will never totally parent their child; and adoptees will never be totally parented by their adoptive parents.** (There are no "as if" pretenses allowed).

3. **Birthparents remain a part of the adoptee's life** whether physically separated or reunited.

Adoption Is a Lifetime Experience

The first reality acknowledges that escaping into the home after the child's placement does not erase how the family was formed. Although the temptation exists to forget the entire adoption process, such forgetting is potentially harmful to the child and to the family structure. Given the need and drive for candor in relationships today, adoptive parents have a responsibility to tell the child he was adopted and to subsequently keep communication channels open. Information from the adoption experience belongs, in part, to the child and his evolving identity. This requires a conscious commitment by the couple not to forget, and a resource commitment from adoption intermediaries and post-adoption programs (post-adoption programs offer the ongoing educational and counseling support necessary when one acknowledges that adoption is a lifetime experience).

The following letter from Bob and Linda was written shortly after their daughter was placed in their arms. Feelings expressed to their daughter's birthmother demonstrate their commitment to base their relationship on truth and openness. They know that for the five people involved (birthparents, adoptive parents, and child) adoption is a lifetime experience:

Dear Special Person,

Through this letter we hope to communicate some of our feelings at this very special time of our lives. Although we realize there is no way we could ever express all the great joy we have experienced since adopting our precious little girl.

We always wanted children, but discovered we would not be biological parents. We knew we would love a child—being biological wasn't important. After being accepted by the agency, we were excited and filled with anticipation. We made all necessary preparations—wallpapered nursery, bought furnishings, took a child care course, read parenting materials, and anxiously waited for our special day. By this time we knew we would have a baby soon and we knew we would love this child. But, we never realized how much!

Our little adopted girl is our whole world. We can't imagine life without her. She has enriched our lives so much. We feel she is the perfect child for us. We are very much a family. She is ours and we are hers. In addition to all our love, she is loved by four grandparents, who are all young and actively involved in her life. . . .

At this happy time in our lives, we realize that this is a difficult time of your life. Upon placement we cried many tears of joy for us and tears of sadness for you. We know you sacrificed you own feelings for your child's future. You are truly a special person. Our daughter will know she's adopted and will know you are out there somewhere. She will only hear positive things about you. She will never be told that you did not want her or love her, rather it was because you loved her so much that you gave her up. There will always be a special place in our hearts for you. You are a special person. God bless and keep you always.

Love,
Parents of An Angel

Adoptive Parents Will Never Totally Parent

The second reality—never being able to totally parent the

adoptee—is initially the hardest to present to adopting parents. Introducing this concept always produces the same startled and defensive comment, "What do you mean TOTALLY parent?"

Not being able to totally parent does not say anything about the adoptive couple's ability to love or be "together people." There are no first or second-best parents in this human experience. There are only adoptive parents who can never give their biological heritage or genetic future to their child and birthparents who cannot raise a child born to them. Both sets of parents in reality experience an incompleteness and loss. The child, in turn, can never be parented by *one set* of parents. He needs the adoptive set to provide the nurturing and shaping part of parenthood. He needs the biological set to provide his genetic past and future.

An adoptive couple's initial defensiveness to the idea that they may not be total parents stems in part from their own belief that the child's birthparents are not only the child's "real" parents, but also the "complete" parents. "Complete" refers to the ability of the birthparents to have successfully reproduced themselves. The uniquely important experience of passing on one's family genes is, of course, not duplicated in the adoptive family structure.

Our discussions with adoptive couples concerning this aspect of the realities focus on how lack of a blood-bond to the adoptee can lead parents to feel sadness, fear, and anger at times. Couples have described experiences of feeling like second-best parents. A parent who feels he is somehow second-best to his child's birthparents and other real parents in this world is apt to put his need to compete with the birthparents above the child's need for knowledge about his heritage. This same adoptive parent may unconsciously seek to totally possess the child instead of helping him integrate information about his birthparents into his growing self-concept.

When adoption intermediaries or well-intentioned friends attempt to minimize for adoptive parents the importance of genetically related birthparents, both parents and children are the real losers. Such statements as, "the nurturing part of parenting is the BEST part of parenthood," are unjust because they encourage adoptive parents to remain defensive. If adoptive parents experience competitive feelings towards birthparents, we believe these feelings are best explored before they adopt. This allows adoptive parents to develop greater insight into themselves and the true importance of their role.

Samantha and Charles, a young adoptive couple, understand and accept this second reality. No matter how hard they may wish, they will never totally parent their son, Jimmy. They can, however, be secure with themselves as Jimmy's parents—secure enough to invite Jimmy's birthmother, Candace, to be a part of their life. Candace, in turn, writes the following letter. All five people in this adoption drama win because they were helped to deal with their initial fears, and then to grow through open communication and trust. Jimmy now has access to both sets of parents:

> Samantha and Charles,
>
> I want to thank you for the beautiful ceramic box. I really love it. I was very excited when I was told I had a letter from you and don't worry it was worth waiting for.
>
> I am so glad Jimmy is doing so well. I have always been told that adopted children take on characteristics of their adoptive parents or I should say parents. I think Jimmy will grow up that way. I hope you are keeping a baby book on him. I think that adds something. I know I'm prejudiced, but he is the handsomest boy in the world. If I ever have any more children he will still be my prettiest one.
>
> My life is passing by in an unremarkable way. I am trying to sort out my life and see where I am going. So far it isn't very far. I am planning on school. The next semester is June which is a long time from now.
>
> Do you know what is very difficult? I work in a Pediatrics office and everyone brings their babys here. Maybe God chose this for me to help me over the rough spots. I can't hide here. I still feel very

comfortable with what has happened. I don't really feel cheated. Sort of detached is a better way of saying it.

I should tell you I had hardly any hair until I was almost two. Now I sit on it. It grows very quickly. I also have a very bad temper and when I was younger I could not control it. I use to do the whole bit of laying on the floor and kicking. And people learn very quickly not to cross me. I am much better now and I am sure Jimmy will out grow his. By the way, I have never been able to sleep while in a moving vehicle, plane or car. I sleep only when not moving. Maybe Jimmy is that way. I am so glad the family enjoyed him.

I have everything from the time Jimmy was in the hospital. I have an envelope that I keep everything in. Your letters and pictures are there.

Well you two take care of each other and Jimmy. I hope things go well.

Love,
Candace

Birthparents Remain a Part of the Adoptee's Life

We often hear adoptive parents say that simply telling the child he was adopted is all they felt was necessary. The idea of mentioning birthparents or the concept that the child would be curious had not occurred to them. The third reality is thus designed to equip adoptive parents with this essential information.

The fact that birthparents remain a part of the adoptee's life. whether physically separated or reunited, emphasizes the bond that exists between a child and his birthparents. Whether described as a family connection or blood tie, adoptees tell us that this bond plays a role in their lives. Some adoptees speak of this role as merely an intellectual curiosity about their background, while others verbalize an emotional drive to have physical contact with a blood relative. At either extreme, the adoptee would like to be able to share his feelings with his adoptive parents. The adoptive parents, however, can both envy and fear the importance of this blood bond to their child, which may make communication difficult or impossible.

Adoptees frequently mention the importance of such simple questions as what their birthparents' personalities were like, what were their interests, what did they look like, but most especially, "Did my birthparents love me?" It is our belief that adoptive parents have a duty to convey whatever facts they know. In addition, it is the responsibility of the adoptive parents to let the adoptee know that they are comfortable in answering his questions—that in fact they expect him to ask questions. Failure to freely communicate may prevent the adoptee from exploring his identity. Whereas, a comfortable, open attitude may prevent a great deal of anxiety and guilt.

Once again, our approach is to introduce to the adoptive parents the reality of the birthparents' continued role in the adoptee's life, and then assist them to understand how that role and their role merge in the child's life. Adoptive parents who are comfortable with this last reality make a double achievement. Because they are capable of empathizing with the child's need to know his blood bond, they will not feel the pain of rejection if he does decide to search for his birthparents. Most important, the adoptive parents can free the adoptee from any disquieting yearning about himself, and possibly earn the reward of being his favored lifetime partners in all his important searches.

LEARNING THROUGH LETTERS

Letter exchanges make it possible for adopting couples to shape and resolve their feelings about the realities of their parental status. We find they write about who they are today and how their infertility experience and adoption struggle helped them grow and mature. They also face their greatest fear—their child's birthparents—in an open manner. As adoptive parents share their life with these birthparents, they come to understand how and why birthparents are a part of the adoptee's life. They also demonstrate confidence in themselves which is then reflected in a relaxed and loving family unit. For example, Rob and Elaine had been married thirteen years before becoming adoptive parents. The period of *becoming* parents held times of real depression for them both. In the following excerpts from the letter they wrote shortly after placement, they share with their child's birth-mother their struggle not only to assume their role but also to accept it:

Dear Birth Mother,

We were so happy to receive your nice letter and it will be saved for our daughter. Even though we have not met you we are united in a deep bond of love with you for this beautiful child. Her birth into this world is one of the most wonderful events that has ever happened. The events in all of our lives that have taken place within the past year will provide new and even more beautiful meanings as time goes by. We know that life can be very difficult at times for each of us and we know so clearly from personal experiences what it is like to struggle and suffer and ask ourselves why we have to go through such times. We now believe that these events are part of a process of learning, growing and developing into stronger persons than we may have ever dreamed was possible for us. Because of this precious child's life we all find new meanings to the word love. We want you to know that there has never been a child born that is more dearly loved nor one who has brought more joy into a home than this little girl. We believe you made very mature and good decisions. We also believe that the Lord is guiding your life and making it possible for you to experience and have a wonderful life filled with love.

We share your great love and respect for this child's life. Since she came into our lives many wonderful and surprising things have taken place. Family, friends and acquaintances from all over the country have written to us—special notes have even been written just for her. She has been given many, many lovely toys, clothes and things that a baby needs. We never expected such an overwhelming outpouring of friendship and love from so many people. It has truly been a thrilling and exciting experience. This is one of the reasons why we say that her life has already shown us love and what wonderful love there is in this world. . . .

We are very proud and happy to be her Mother and Father, and we believe you can be proud also. We wish to have you understand and to feel the great sense of satisfaction, joy and love that her life has brought to us. It is not possible to say in one letter what a miracle she is to us.

We pray for you and want you to have faith, joy and love in your life, increasing as time goes by. We send you our love and our very best wishes for a wonderful life.

Love,
The Adoptive Parents

Another couple, Patricia and Fred, wrote three letters to their child's birthmother within the first three years. Their third letter demonstrates their evolution and final acceptance of the realities involved in adoption. They reached this point by continuing to read books on adoption, by attending workshops about adoption, by remaining active in an adoptive parent support group, as well as by going through the adoption process again for a second child:

Dear Birthmother,

Greetings! I was so happy to hear from our social worker that you and she had spoken. I am so glad that all is well with you. I will try to bring you up to date on the happenings in this last year. It has been a hectic one since we are now the parents of two daughters. As you can imagine, being the parents of two is more complicated plus hectic than being the parents of one!

We have really enjoyed watching the love

develop between the two sisters. As the older and more mature sister, Katherine gives the baby lots of guidance, loving care, and needless to say, bossing! Katherine knows how to feed her and does try to be helpful whenever she gets a chance or whenever she's in the mood for it. . . .

It has been terrific to watch Katherine's development and reasoning ability. She is extremely intelligent and quick. She talks in complete sentences and has done so for over a year. Her vocabulary is excellent—she uses words like delicate, initiated and wonderful. She has good command of shades of meanings and abstract words. . . .

I am enclosing some pictures for you. I will get some more duplicated for you. Please do be patient, tho, because it usually takes me awhile to do things these days.

I really appreciate your being willing to fill out the form our agency has devised for sharing additional information. I want you to know that we would love to hear any and all details about you and your family. We want Katherine to feel there is continuity in her life and we don't want her heritage to be a mystery. As I have learned more about adoption I have come to realize how important all this is. We would love to have names, birthdates, places of birth, pictures and anything else you feel like sharing about you, your family, and anyone else you feel would feature as important in Katherine's life. She is so attuned to adoption that it's just terrific. When she was about 2 1/2 she pensively asked me "Mommy, my birthmother, she not know me?" I went on to explain that you did know her at birth and that you did spend time with her. Isn't it amazing how quickly children grasp information?!

Well, as you can see I can go on and on about Katherine. . . .

We think of you often and feel so fortunate that we are Katherine's parents. She is a joy! And

I am sure that some day you will have the opportunity to see that first hand. As our social worker mentioned to you if ever you would like to talk on the phone or in person with me, I would be very delighted to meet you. It would be marvelous to be able to share with Katherine personal contact with you. Again, it takes the mystery out of adoption and truly personalizes it. For as someone (an adoptive parent) recently wrote to her child's birthmother "Tho he is our child now, he will never stop being your child too." We feel that way too. I want you to know that as long as you want a yearly letter regarding Katherine, that I will be very happy to write you one. I must admit that it is fun to go on and on about her!

Stay well. We too would love to hear from you and do stay in touch.

All the best to you.

With great fondness,
Patricia

Through the letter exchange, couples like Rob and Elaine and Patricia and Fred find themselves not fearing some invisible birthparent. Instead, adoptive parents speak in caring terms of "our" birthparents. As a result, couples naturally progress from a need to pretend that the child was born to them to an acceptance of the adoptive family structure as it is.

Adoption is not a onetime event that otherwise mimics biological parenthood. There are differences—differences that do not have to overpower any couple if openly and honestly managed. Since we have used this approach, we have seen the struggle to accept infertility end in both growth and peace for our adoptive parents.

6

The Adoption Intermediary: Preparing the New Parents

It's my child's birthday today
I have no memories of the pain and struggle, as he
entered this life
As he fought for his first breath
I have no memories of his life growing inside of me
and fighting to be released
I have no memories from the beginning months of
his life.
Another "someone" was there—Another "someone"
*suffered for my joy . . . **

Today's intermediary in the adoption process is doing a significantly better job than ever before—but there is still much to be done. The work is too crucial to leave to half measures and happenstance. Let's start with our philosophy of the intermediary role:

> The professional adoption counselor, agency, doctor, or lawyer provides not just a mechanical function of placing a child (or facilitating the placement), but must be an aid in *preparing* the adoptive parents and birthparents for a new role. Furthermore, the intermediary must empower the adoptive parents (and birthparents) to be in control of the adoption. We firmly believe *all* of the decisions and choices must be in the hands of the parties involved, not the adoption intermediary. The intermediary role must be one of providing counseling, education, and support, rather than control and decision making.

*From "A Birthday," reprinted with permission of the author from Adoption Triangle Ministry.

In this chapter, we will explore how we have applied the above ideology to our work with prospective adoptive parents. Later, in Chapter 7, we will examine this philosophy in reference to our adoptive practices with birthparents.

BEYOND SCREENING: COUNSELING AND HOME STUDY

Couples readily seek an intermediary to adopt a child, but less commonly to obtain assistance in integrating their role as adoptive parents. Knowing the dual purpose of an intermediary, responsible intermediaries must help the potential adoptive parents in both areas and not serve simply as a "screening" agency. Regrettably, traditional adoptive home studies revolve only around the screening process and the suitability of the prospective parents as parents. Investigation of the home and family circumstances all too often leave off before making the most important inquiry. Areas unique to adoptive parenthood are often neglected in the search for a "perfect couple."

One prospective adoptive couple, Martin and Sheila, had been "approved" for adoption by two agencies within the past two years. Each time, Martin and Sheila moved to another area before a child could be placed with them. In reading the completed home studies from these other two well-known agencies, we discovered thorough descriptions of the couple, their personalities, marital adjustments, family background, and experience with children. We found no references to how Martin and Sheila would tell their child he was adopted, how they felt about the unique responsibilities of adoptive parenthood, or what they thought or felt toward the potential birthparents of their child. In short, neither agency had discussed adoption.

Martin is an attorney and Sheila is a nurse and both admit they believed the intermediary's sole objective was to screen and approve of them as parents. They did not see beyond the baby stages of diapers and feeding. They did not anticipate, nor did the intermediary alert them, to the time when the inevitable issues of adoptive parenthood would arise. Martin and Sheila were even unaware that the role of an adoptive parent required additional preparation. Like most couples, Martin and Sheila did not know any other adoptive couples who might have answered questions or served as role models. Actually, their entire knowledge and experience about adoption consisted of the four myths plus the unusual but scarcely enlightening experience of what we can only characterize as two superficial studies into their suitability to adopt a child.

Martin and Sheila are typical. The intermediary—whether professional counselor, agency, family physician, or lawyer—is approached by two vulnerable individuals who possess limited or faulty insight into the implications of the role they seek. Adoption, to these frustrated potential parents, may be their only way to get a child and to regain control of their lives and destinies. They do not know the realities of adoption; and they certainly do not know the questions that will be most important to prepare them to be effective adoptive parents.

When the professional intermediary merely places a child with such a "perfect couple," the intermediary effectively encourages the couple to consider the child "as if" he were theirs by natural birth. As we point out in Chapter 5, forgetting the differences in how the family was formed is an understandable adaptation to a long and painful infertility experience. Besides, without trained intermediary assistance and support, the adopting parents learn no other options.

If this couple is later introduced to the realities of adoption, they will be surprised and frightened. No knowledgeable intermediary is there to explain or reassure, and the realities, which we have already discussed, are blunt:

1. Adoption is a lifetime experience.

2. Adoptive parents will never totally parent their child; and adoptees will never be totally parented by their adoptive parents.

3. Birthparents remain a part of the adoptee's life whether physically separated or reunited.

These realities, combined with the misconceptions of the myths and any unresolved issues around infertility, create a dissonance that makes moving toward open ideas very difficult, if not insurmountable.

In contrast, our work with prospective adoptive parents acknowledges that the burden of preparing these parents for their new role rests always with the intermediary. We believe that the primary role of the intermediary is to provide counseling, education about adoption issues and realities, and support. We want our couples to explore their stereotypes, misconceptions, and apprehensions before they become parents.

Our first objective is to expose the four myths of adoption as harmful and stultifying. We recommend beginning this process at the Orientation Meeting, which is the adopting couple's initial introduction to the realities in adoption. This session explores the myths and realities in adoption, as well as the benefits of open adoption.

Couples who enter our adoption program attend an intensive two-session adoption workshop. This workshop typically includes eight to ten prospective adoptive couples and a group leader. The group leader acts as a facilitator since the workshop stresses group exploration and discussion, not lectures. Activities are designed to allow all participants to examine feelings about their infertility experience and their beliefs about birthparents. Required reading also expands the couple's awareness of adoption issues.

Initial discussions, for example, explore the attitudes of our prospective parents about the role they are seeking—adoptive parenthood. Where are they in the process of resolving infertility? Is this baby to be a substitute for the natural child they have been denied? Do they believe genuine parenthood is the child-bearing-and-rearing type only? What do they know about adoption? Which of the four myths do they believe? Which of the four myths do their parents and friends believe? This discussion area acknowledges the differences between biological and adoptive parenthood, and initiates an inspection by all participants of their own attitudes towards adoption and themselves as adoptive parents.

An important aspect of the workshop focuses on understanding the birthparents. Do our adopting couples imagine the birthmother as a ''tramp,'' and the birthfather as "irresponsible?" How will they tell their child his birthparents were unmarried? Does it matter to them, to their family, to their friends that the child may be illegitimate? Discussions stress that each adoptive parent's feelings toward the birthparents will affect the child's evolving self-image.

We climax our introduction to the realities of birthparents through a panel of actual birthmothers who have placed their babies for adoption. These birthmothers talk about their feelings towards pregnancy, their decision to place their babies for adoption, their ongoing relationship with the adoptive family and child, and each one's love for her child. This leads to couples asking the birthmothers further questions about their experiences. This dialogue is undoubtedly the richest part of the workshop and something the couples vividly remember.

The following letter from Bob expresses some of his initial apprehensions about open adoption and his personal evolution as the result of the workshop experience:

> My only reason for selecting an open adoption was to get a baby. The closed systems no longer had children readily available, and after six years of the infertility circus my wife and I wanted a lovely little baby right now. Other than that I had no reason for choosing an open adoption as an option. The whole concept of "open" seemed too radical and unstable for my more traditional concept of adoption—"give me the child, seal the records, and get lost." The fact that the child had birthparents was irrelevant to me. Their presence represented more of a liability to me than an asset, a threat more than anything. What if they changed their mind? What if they want to come and see the baby? Do they want to spend Christmas with us? Why don't they just go away? Will my child love me if the birthparents are around? My selfish and narrow minded hostility to these questions almost prevented me from adopting my little daughter Kate.
>
> I was blinded by the idea that I knew all about adoption. Little did I realize that I was prejudging

the entire process without taking the time to understand the nature of adoption itself. Fortunately, the Independent Adoption Center required that I participate in a series of sessions structured to familiarize me with the many aspects of open adoption. It was at these sessions that I began to realize how narrow my thinking was and how many of the things I was most fearful of were simply rooted in mistrust, lack of control, and ignorance. My fears were dissipated by the many people who spoke about their happiness and success. They made me see that the more open the adoption the greater the benefit for all concerned.

By knowing the birthparents I will be able to deal openly with the many questions that will inevitably be faced. Medical information only begins to scratch the surface of what I need to know. I began to realize that by pretending that there are no birthparents, or that ignorance was bliss, I was building a new life and family on a lie. I could not make a biological family out of an adoptive one, and that was an unpalatable truth to accept.

Lastly I had to respect the birthparents' desire to place this child in a home of their choosing. Adoption was a choice that they wanted. Ironically we were all on the same side, solving each others problem. As for the little requests by a birthmother to come and see the baby once in a while, well that was no longer the threat it used to be. Once I made the effort to understand the birthmother's desire to have this adoption succeed, that's when I realized how small a request she was making. She was giving us a gift for a lifetime. Her decision made possible a dream of ours that all the science in the world could not satisfy. Once I appreciated how much she was doing for us, I found it hard not to have the compassion and love to care for her needs, too.

The workshop is designed to sensitize participants to how their own infertility experience will play a part in their role as adoptive parents. In addition, activities are designed to illustrate how their myths, stereotypes, or expectations could shape their judgments about birthparents and adoptees. Couples often begin the workshop convinced that anyone who gives away a child could not love that child (first myth), and neither wants nor deserves information about the child (third myth). Many couples at this stage freely admit that they fear the birthparents as a threat to the family unit they so desperately desire. This mixture of misconceptions, untruths, and anxieties is revealed and discussed during the workshop.

This next sensitive letter was written by Hugh and Jane to their son's birthmother. The letter is significant because Hugh had entered the workshop with strong negative preconceptions about all birthparents. His attitude is familiar: "What right does she have to information? After all, she obviously did not want the baby; she gave it away." In contrast, their letter demonstrates an ability to empathize with the birthmother after only a short exposure to the birthparent's perspective:

> Dear Birth Mother of Our Son,
>
> Through the grace of God, you brought a precious son into this world. His life has already brought so much joy to so many! If things are truly planned, this could not have been more perfectly planned. He has fit into our lives as if it was always meant to be. He has also brought so much happiness to our families and friends. There has been more excitement over this beautiful child than we have ever seen for such an important occasion.
>
> Most importantly, we want you to know what a wonderfully beautiful little person he is. Our son is growing in all ways—physically, emotionally, intellectually and spiritually. We know we have someone in our home that we will be a tremendous influence on, but we will do the very best we can to raise him as an individual in his own right.
>
> Our son is a very happy little guy, with a sunny disposition. His smile and laugh is worth more than

all the riches in the world. He is healthy, well-adjusted, very alert, attentive, and strong. He babbles, coos, talks, sings, and blows millions of happy bubbles! He notices everything around him with great interest, and loves to go outdoors and take walks in his stroller.

We sit with him in our laps and look at books with him, and he is already fascinated. We listen to a lot of music, and deep-voiced singing is his favorite. In the car we play a Harry Chapin tape he is especially attentive to. . . . Thank you for all the gifts you sent (though, here those words seem too small!). We will keep all of them as wonderful remembrances. The night light is burning continuously by his crib. The mobile is just beautiful, and fits perfectly in his bright, sunny room. Please thank your friend for it.

Yes, he was born in the year of the Child, and came to us in the year of the Family. We want you to know that he will know he had a birthmother who loved him very much. Thank you from his adoptive parents who love him more than words can ever say. Thank you for giving him life—thank you for entrusting that life to us. We love him truly for himself, and we love you.

Our son will be baptised on Easter Sunday—what a perfect time for this child of God!

May God bless and keep you. May you find joy and love in this world, and know the joy and love you have given others. You will always be in our hearts and prayers; please remember us in yours. You are very special. You gave us all something no one else could.

Love from all of us,
His Adoptive Parents

Finally, the workshop focuses on some other adoption realities and on the remaining individual in the adoption drama—the adoptee. Our objectives at this point are two. The first objective is to create an encouraging and supportive atmosphere so the adoptive parents may examine any unconscious needs to compete with the child's birthparents. This drive to compete often masquerades in the second myth (secrecy is the only way) and fourth myth (adoptees should not search). Our objective is to uncover the competitiveness and provide information to show that adoptive parents are not second-best parents.

In addition, we assist these prospective parents to leave behind the tendency to see and believe what they want to see and believe, especially the "as if he were born to me" adaptation. With support from a group atmosphere, we present the three primary realities of adoption: This is a life-time commitment; you are not the adoptee's only parents; and birthparents remain part of your life because they are a part of the adoptee.

Our second objective is to help participants prepare the child to face life with an open, informed, relaxed acceptance of the fact he was adopted. Adoption should be a natural and comfortable subject in the home. If the adoptee grows up always knowing he was adopted, he will consider the subject commonplace. Results may be quite different, however, if he learns of his adoptive status for the first time at later periods of emotional development.

Throughout this session, adoptive parents are shown how their attitudes will reflect in their communications to their child. The dynamics are simple. As the child begins to question the adoption process and his "other parents," adoptive parents can once again become unsure of their worth as parents and angry at these mysterious birthparents. Parents so hurt and threatened may answer questions in such a way as to block further questions. If mother stumbles with her answer and tears come to her eyes, the adoptee quickly gets the message not to ask.

Young children unable to talk about adoption will often display anxieties, nightmares, fantasies, or behavioral problems. In addition, we often meet adoptive parents of older adoptees who say, "My child doesn't want to know anything. He is perfectly content." Sadly, their son may be actively but secretly searching for his birthparents but unable to share his search with his parents because he does not want to hurt them. Open communication in the home can eliminate or reduce these problems for both young and older adoptees. Therefore, through the workshop experience we teach our parents that open communication must be a conscious goal of each adoptive parent.

As mentioned earlier, adoptive parents tend to forget how the adoptee came into their family once they become a family unit. The stage could thus be set for these parents not to tell the adoptee at all. Allison, an adoptive mother who is herself an adoptee, understands the perils involved. She remembers growing up, "always knowing I was adopted." She plans on her son also having all the information he will need: "I hope that we will be able to make him feel as secure in our love for him as my parents made me feel." Allison wrote this reassuring letter to the birthmother of her son:

> To the Birth Mother of Our Son,
> First, I would like to thank you for the very beautiful letters you sent to us and our son. I know that someday they will be very meaningful to him and will help him to understand his adoption.
> I would like to tell you a little about myself. I, too, was adopted. I was born in San Antonio. However, since my Dad was in the service I spent most of my growing years all over the world. Our family is extremely close knit. I have a brother and sister, also adopted. Our parents are truly wonderful people and we have always felt very loved and very secure. My mother and father were very open and honest with us about the circumstances of our adoption. I never felt that I was unwanted and I know that my son will understand why you could not care for him. . . .
> I have so many feelings I would like to express to you. Compassion—I know your decision to give your baby up for adoption was a difficult one. I admire your courage and respect you for doing what you felt to be in the best interest of your baby. I am extremely grateful to you for giving us a beautiful son for our own. . . .

His disposition couldn't be better. He seldom gets fussy or cries. He's just a happy little baby. I can attribute his disposition in part to the peace you felt with yourself during your pregnancy. Your letters seemed to convey that you were peaceful with your decision. We take him everywhere and he is always good. For Thanksgiving, we took him to Dallas to meet my husband's family. They were thrilled with him and each one took their turn holding him and bouncing him on their knee. For Christmas he met my side of the family. My mother was the only one who saw him right away and she came as soon as we got him. His homecoming was her birthday. The whole family was quite taken with him and his grandfather just sat and marvelled at him. . . .

What else can I tell you? From the very first moment that I held him, I loved him and felt he was mine. Each day that I wake up and look at him, I can hardly believe it. Our love for him grows stronger each day and we enjoy watching him develop.

I have saved all the information and papers regarding his adoption and birth to place in a scrapbook. I intend to put it in storybook form, so that he will have his own little story. I hope that we will be able to make him feel as secure in our love for him as my parents made me feel.

I could go on and on, but there are really not enough appropriate words to express my feelings. I love our beautiful son and I will have a special place in my heart for the woman who made my dreams become a reality.

Thank you.

The workshop ends with a role-playing exercise designed to introduce the couples to questions an adopted child might ask. Questions range from a three-year-old asking, "Was I in your tummy, Mommy?" to a six-year-old asking "Why did my 'real' Mommy give me up?" The role-playing prevents the couples from simply intellectualizing about adoption and instead directs energies to the difficult experiences of actually sharing information with the child.

The entire workshop is an emotional experience for adopting couples. The group leader must remain creative in order to facilitate interaction by everyone. This effort requires a commitment of time and energy by the adoption intermediary. The work is rewarded by the growth and happiness experienced by the couples, and vividly demonstrated in their letters:

> To the Mother of our Dear Child,
>
> While this letter is not hard to write in the sense that you are our baby's natural mother, it is difficult in the respect that we could never be able to put down on paper the absolute happiness and joy he has brought to us. As we write this letter in the early morning, he is lying between us on the bed gurgling and laughing and enjoying us as we enjoy him. He is without a doubt the sweetest thing on this earth, and we fear he will be just a little bit spoiled but we're not going to worry about that. He's the first grandchild and the first niece or nephew for four of his uncles and aunt; he's the star of the show wherever he goes. We're lucky also that three of our dearest friends have children close to his age or will have children within the next several months—so he'll be part of a loving family and close friendships. His grandfather stops by every morning on his way to work to bring him a freshly cut rose and to play with him.
>
> I hope this letter doesn't sound disjointed or rambling, but there are so many things we'd like to relate to you that they just seem to come in flashes.
>
> To sum up his characteristics—if there is a cuter or smarter baby than he, a person would be hard pressed to find him or her. A little parental pride showing through but we feel that way. We don't want to sound gushy, but he is just about the

sweetest thing to happen to us.

We know how difficult it was for you to part with him, and your letter touched us deeply. We believe that someone with your sensitivity and love must have passed that to your child, and we will be eternally grateful. You may not know how someone can love a child who is not theirs naturally, but rest assured it seems to be the most natural thing of all—loving a sweet and beautiful innocent. The minute we saw him at the agency, it was love at first sight and it has grown by leaps and bounds.

We were raised in close loving families and we know the value of love and its overt expressions, so we take every opportunity to hold, hug, or kiss him— it's so easy to do with him.

In ending this letter, we would want you to know that he is secure and loved and will be for the rest of our lives.

Sincerely yours,

The Adoptive Parents

A POST-ADOPTION COMMITMENT

During the post-placement stage, couples are encouraged to attend regularly scheduled post-birth group counseling sessions. These sessions, which are led by a counselor, focus again on adoption issues and realities—now from the perspective of actually being adoptive parents and having "real" birthparents to relate to.

Even that does not end our story. We work to keep couples involved with the adoption center after their adoption is final. Through a volunteer alumni group, we sponsor an annual family picnic (which many adoptive parents attend with their birthmother), annual banquet, and numerous other family activities throughout the year (e.g., a trip to the zoo, Easter egg hunt, etc.). The picnic, as well as other family activities, serves to bring couples back together to proudly show off their children and to jointly celebrate their happiness.

We also encourage adoptive families to become volunteers with our organization. Volunteers serve a variety of capacities, including office work, transporting birthmothers to the office for counseling appointments, housing a birthmother, etc. Through interaction with adoptive parents, birthmothers see what an adoptive family is like while still making their own decisions about adoption; and in turn, the families gain valuable further understanding of birthparents. Sally, an adoptive mother, wrote about her experience volunteering with one birthmother, who was living in a maternity home:

AN OPEN LETTER FROM A VOLUNTEER FAMILY

I was asked to write this to share my experience with other adoptive families. My husband and I are a volunteer family for the girls at the maternity home. We were assigned to one girl and became friends during her last two months of pregnancy. We picked her up once a week and brought her into our home for dinner and friendship. I became very close to her. She asked for me to be with her when she relinquished her baby. I agreed and my heart broke. To see the hurt in her face and heart was very upsetting to me. I know that she was really doing the best thing for her baby, still I got very emotionally confused. It is hard to imagine the pain these girls go through when they sign their name to that piece of paper. After a good cry she seemed at peace with herself, knowing her baby would have a much better life. Before she left to go home she said again she knew she had done the right thing. Seeing her that way helped me with my emotions.

The agency needs families to volunteer for the Volunteer Family Program. Believe me, it is a very rewarding experience. One day a week is not much compared to what these girls have given us. If it were not for them we (adoptive families) would not have that bundle of joy to rock and sing to.

Sally

P.S. To the family who got this girl's baby let me
say, she loved that baby very much and took very
good care of herself. You have a very special baby!

We also see the need for agencies and other adoption
organizations to focus on post-finalization services. Ongoing
workshops and support groups should be available for adoptive parents, birthparents, adoptees, and interested professionals to help each face questions and problems in dealing
with adoption in the years after the child's placement. We
are very pleased to know resources are available today to
deal with the realities of adoption. In many ways, we see
forward-looking adoption intermediaries agreeing with Lor-
raine, the adoptive mother who wrote the following in a letter
to her son's birthmother:

. . . God, through you and our son's birthfather, has
answered our prayers in bringing to us a bright
ray of sunshine in the form of our sweet little boy.
We all share a special bond . . . we will have each
given of ourselves to the creation of this very special little person.

7

The Adoption Intermediary: Preparing the Birthparents

Fly away—fly away
Never to return
I've lost
and you've gained.

There's an empty feeling deep inside
A warm spot—growing cold
These feelings I've accepted
Hoping one day they be filled.

Fly away—fly away
Never to return
I've lost
And you've gained.

There was an empty feeling deep inside
Now a cold spot—growing warm
These feelings being accepted
Gaining happiness and love.

> D. L. Click
> Birthmother

Birthparents confronted with an unplanned pregnancy face both the stress of an immediate crisis and the possibility of lifetime pain. For the birthmother three options challenge her, each emotionally charged:

"Do I seek an abortion?"

"Do I give birth and then raise my child?"

"Do I place my child for adoption?"

Birthfathers and immediate family members also deal with each of these alternatives but from a perspective more physically removed. Adoption is only one of the alternatives for all these individuals, and not necessarily the "only good and reasonable choice." Contrary to the overwhelming belief in the myths of adoption that say birthparents "do not care" and birthparents "will and should forget," birthparents care deeply for the life they create. The decision to relinquish that life for someone else to parent is an unforgettable decision. This decision can result in a lifetime of grief and despair, the trauma of which some birthparents have described as "a psychological amputation." Therefore, the adoption intermediary has the responsibility, when approached, to understand the dynamics of an unplanned pregnancy. Assisting birthparents to explore all three options without placing value judgments on any one decision is the intermediary's duty and challenge.

Birthparents are capable of emotional maturation in confronting, coping, and growing with the unplanned pregnancy. This growth usually requires professional aid both in making an unhurried and informed decision, and then in accepting the chosen alternative. The adoption intermediary must have the skill, training, and time required to accomplish such professional counseling. Resource commitment for this process is costly. Therefore, the adoption intermediary might be tempted to accept a birthparent's initial approach and first decision. Counseling that points only to adoption certainly requires less time and energy. The end result of such narrow counseling also appears the same—an adoptive placement which makes two adoptive parents happy. The birthparents, however, may not be so happy. Once again, we emphasize that birthparents are not faceless, unfeeling baby machines who "will forget in time." Birthparents do not turn off their responsibility and love upon the signing of relinquishment papers.

The following two letters were written by one such birthmother, named Kristin. Her letters to her baby and the adoptive parents detail her experience with an unplanned pregnancy, delivery, and feelings after her baby's adoption:

Dear Beautiful People,
    I just found out today that you received my baby. I don't know you and I don't know if our paths

will ever cross in life, but I want you to know that
I am eternally grateful to you, and I love you both
with all my heart. It is really strange. We are so
distant, but yet I feel so close to you, I know you
people are gifts from God. My giving up this baby
was the hardest thing in my life that I have ever
done, but it was because I have loved her so much
that I made my decision. I want her to have the
kind of raising that I had, two loving parents that
could provide her with the spiritual, emotional and
material needs that are involved with raising a child
The main thing being two parents that love her,
which is something I couldn't provide by myself.
Don't get me wrong, I could smother her with love,
but there is so much more to it than that that I
know you can provide for her. I hope you don't mind
me referring to her as "my" baby, I realize I gave
her up legally, and she is yours, but I do have mater-
nal feelings toward her. I hope you understand what
I'm trying to say.

I'd like to share my life while pregnant and
the delivery with you. I had no morning sickness
with her, it was a perfect pregnancy, no problems
whatsoever. I have always been "healthy" (plump—I
don't like that word) so you couldn't really tell I
was pregnant until about my seventh month. I just
looked like I was gaining weight. I first felt her
kick when I was about 5-1/2 months. It's really a
neat feeling. As I got further along in the pregnancy, the harder she kicked. You could see it from
the outside. If I placed both hands flat on my abdo-
men, I could feel her moving around. At night I
would usually sleep on my side, and she would sink
to the side against the bed. When I got out of bed,
I would have to check my balance because my lop-
sided stomach made me clumsy.

What else can I tell you—towards the end, she
would sleep all day, and move around most of the
night, much to my despair (ha ha). She was due
on January 11, but as you know was born January

24. That was the longest two weeks. To me it seemed longer than the whole pregnancy.

During the morning of January 23, I woke up with slight cramps, so I figured time was getting near. During the day they continued. They weren't painful, they felt like menstral cramps. I didn't know what kind of pain to expect. I had always heard that the delivery is painful. As night came, the cramps started coming about every hour lasting about a minute or so. Gradually they came between 20 and 30 minutes apart. It was then I told the dorm mother, but I really wasn't sure because I didn't really hurt as I expected. I was calm throughout the time. I just kept waiting for bad pains but they never came. By midnight the cramps were 10-12 minutes apart, so the dorm mother said we would go to the hospital and let them check me just to make sure. So—we went and got there about 12:30.

The first thing the nurse asked me was if my water broke. When I said no, she said we didn't have to worry. They took me in the prep room and checked to see if I was dialated far enough yet. I measured at 6 cm. The nurse said she didn't believe I was that far along because I was so calm. It was at that time I started thinking "wow, this is really it." I asked how long they thought before the baby would be born and was told probably by 7:00 A.M. Well, they prepped me and my contractions were getting closer and starting to hurt—but still not like I expected. They put me in a room and gave me a shot for pain. I was supposed to be asleep for the delivery—I didn't want to remember it. Anyway, they measured me again. By this time it was about 1:15—I was 8 cm. I had a feeling it was going to be sooner than anticipated. A few minutes later they checked me again and said it was time to be wheeled into delivery. I was wondering when they were going to put me to sleep—I knew they couldn't do it too late. Then, the doctor walked in the room, and said it was too late, so I was awake throughout the entire thing. Now that I think about it, I'm glad I was awake, it all happened too fast. There was one real bad contraction and her head was born, then the rest of her just slid right out. She was laid upon my stomach for a few seconds—feeling her outside and inside is so different, it's such a separation. I remember her scream <u>loud</u> when the doctor slapped her—she has a healthy set of lungs. I was glad it was over, and I was ready to get back to my normal way of life.

The next day I went to see her, and got to hold her. I thought she was beautiful—I hope you do! It really hit me hard, the fact of what I was doing— as I was holding her, looking at her and thinking about her—I started crying. It hurt so much, but I knew what I wanted and what she needed. Even as young as I am, I realize that raising a child is a hard thing to do. There is happiness and there is pain, but you forget the pain because the happiness outweighs it. At this point, I really don't know what else to tell you—I'd like to keep in touch with you and you with me—but only if you want. I don't want you to feel I'm imposing, it's just that I'd like to know how your family is growing together. Also, I'd like to ask you to send me a picture of her in a few months—I'm curious to see what she looks like then, but I'm leaving the decision up to you. Whatever you feel best.

As you grow together in life, I imagine the baby when older will ask questions of her background. I don't know what you will tell her, but I know it will be the right thing. I'm writing her a letter also, and I want you to read it and give it to her when you feel that she is mature enough. If she decides that she wants to find me, please help her and don't feel threatened. I don't want to interfere with your relationship, and I won't do anything or say anything to hinder it. Remember, I love you too!

Well, I said most everything I wanted to so

I'll come to a close. If you have any questions—just let me know, I'm keeping close contact with the agency, and am looking forward to hearing from you. God bless you and your family and may you have a happy and prosperous life.

> Take care!
> I Love You
> Kristin

P.S. I kept this letter for a while trying to decide whether I should add something or leave something out but decided this is what I really feel so I chose to leave it as is.

Today Kristin is a nurse's aide and she looks forward to finishing college, future marriage, and future children. Still, her firstborn daughter is remembered, as much today as she was when Kristin wrote her this letter:

My Daughter,

I really don't know how to begin this letter. There are so many things about you that I would love to know. I imagine your main question is why. I will try to explain that to you along with a few other things from my life.

I hope that by the time you read this, you are old enough to understand my reasoning, and that you don't hold it against me. I don't know what your view on me will be because I'm not adopted. I can only try to wonder what you are feeling. I want you to know how grateful I am to your parents for giving you a life that I couldn't. As I am writing this letter I wonder at what time in your life you will read this. I wonder what you look like, how old you are, what your name is, and all kinds of things. I guess the main thing I wonder about is if you ever want to find me. I want to see you, but then I have to think, I don't know how my life will be later. I only hope the situation will permit it. There is one thing I ask of you. If you do decide

to come look for me, please do it because you really
want to find me, not for some unknown reason.

I'll tell you a bit about your biological background. First your father. He's tall, 6'2", thin, has
black hair, beautiful brown eyes and he's very handsome. He's from Iran, born and raised there. He came
to this country to go to college. He has five brothers
and three sisters, and he's the baby of the family.
He's 18 now. He's a very quiet person, also very
serious. He was going to college for a degree in Chem-
ical Engineering.

As for me, I'm 5'4", on the plump side (not
thin for sure, but not really fat). I have brown hair,
green eyes and I'm real light complected. I'm going
to school for my R.N. and I have two more years
to go. I have one brother, 6 years younger than me.
I am 19. I want you to know your father was the
first person I ever went to bed with. I felt in such
a way for him that I hadn't felt for anyone else.
We had a beautiful friendship at first and then it
grew stronger. We had sex only one time, he never
pressured or pushed me to it, it was by mutual agree-
ment, and I didn't think one time would do any
harm. That day was April 21. It was a few days
before I was to leave college to go home. My parents
never suspected my being pregnant. I knew it deep
inside but I wouldn't admit it to myself. I just denied
it. I hardly showed until I was 8 months pregnant.
When I went back to school, I didn't tell your father.
I knew he planned to go back to his country someday. Well as always, time went on. I had no plans
as of what to do. Two of my best friends knew of
my situation and they found the agency where I
stayed until you were born. Baby, if you are anything like you were when I knew you—carried and
delivered you—I know you are perfect. You never
gave me a minute of trouble. Your delivery was perfect. I was awake and it wasn't painful—that much
anyway. I don't imagine you know it, but we did
have some time together. I watched you enter this

big, wide world and I even got to hold you and feel
you outside of me for a short time.

Your father didn't know anything about you
until afterwards. I told him two months later. He
was very hurt because he thought I was lying to
him. At that time I knew I wouldn't see him again
because he was going back home. I showed him my
picture of you and he looked at it for a long time.
I feel that in time he will accept the fact and I
know that picture will remain in his mind forever.
We parted that night with love and best wishes
for both of us.

So many times now I feel lost. Love hurts very
much, but life goes on and now I'm trying to carry
on with my life. I date different guys, but I'm scared
to get close to anyone. I don't want to lose them.
I guess it will be this way for a while. I'm sure
one day I will meet someone to take his place.

You know I think of you all the time. I see
babies every day and wonder about you. I mentioned
before that I got to hold you. You were beautiful—
dark hair, light skin and bright blue eyes—oh yes
and a beautiful nose. You were so trusting. As I
held you I started crying. I loved and wanted you
so much, but I had nothing. I had seen so many
girls in my situation where it didn't work out, and
I wanted you to have the best chance that life could
give. I have memories of you that I will cherish
forever. So babe, as you go along in life, be thankful
you have the parents you do. They have given you
everything that I couldn't. I brought you into the
world, but they've done the hardest part—watching
you grow, been with you in bad times as well as
good, have helped you, have taken care of you, and
done everything involved in leading a baby into a
mature adult capable of living an adult life. One
day in life, if it is God's will and destiny, we will
meet again, if not we will live our lives to the fullest
and carry on in a way we feel right for us. Just
remember, any decision whether big or small will

affect us in some way for all the days of our lives.
So, baby, you take care of yourself. Do what you
feel you need to do, and live your life the best way
you can. Just be careful, life isn't always easy—
but dwell on the good things. They outweigh the
bad and remember I'll love you, and I'll never forget my first born baby.

Love always,
Kristin

P.S. I'm here if you need me—it's up to you.

Kristin's letters clearly illustrate the deep love birthparents have for their children. Adoptive placement does not
erase those emotions. Adoption intermediaries can no longer
ignore the reality and extent of these feelings by telling birthparents "you will or you should forget" (the third myth). The
professional intermediary must provide the assistance
required for birthparents to effectively resolve the crisis and
consequences of an unplanned pregnancy.

PREGNANCY COUNSELING: THREE PHASES

The birthmother will go through three distinct phases in
an unplanned pregnancy as we view it. The first phase spans
the time from learning about the pregnancy to the birth of
the child. The second phase begins with the birth of the
baby. The third phase occurs after the child is placed in an
adoptive home.

In this chapter, and frequently throughout the book, we
write in terms of the birthmother rather than birthparents
because regrettably the great majority of clients are birthmothers. Birthfathers, not undergoing physical changes, are
capable of denying the reality of a pregnancy longer than
most birthmothers. For that reason, we see fewer fathers. In
addition, we have other access barriers to our birthfathers
which account for our limited exposure to their unique needs.
Nevertheless the birthfathers we have counseled have convinced us that the emotional experiences are the same for
both parents—though they may differ in degree.

We strongly advocate that birthfathers not be forgotten. The adoption myth that sees the birthfather as "irresponsible and uncaring" is widely believed, making it easy for adoption intermediaries to overlook a birthfather's crisis. Without social support or counseling, the birthfather is likely to carry emotional scars as the aftermath of his child's placement. One birthfather told us (some fourteen years after his daughter was adopted) "I'll never have another child. It's the punishment I deserve for giving away my first."

Phase One—Before the Baby is Born

Fear, loneliness, and uncertainty permeate the initial phase of an unplanned pregnancy, lasting until the baby's birth. Counseling sessions in the beginning focus on the immediate crisis that led the birthmother to seek assistance. For some birthmothers this is dealing with how to tell their parents or other significant persons about their pregnancy. In other cases, the problem facing the birthmother is immediate financial need. In a few cases the initial crisis is overcoming a denial of the pregnancy and exploring the feelings that are hidden within the denial system. As we deal with these immediate factors birthmothers begin to examine their guilt about having made a mistake or having disappointed the people they love. Some of our clients at this point will select abortion as their alternative; and if that is their considered option, we assist them through proper referrals.

Once the immediate crisis is resolved, intensive counseling begins. Our goal is for the expectant mother to understand her pregnancy, herself, and the decision she will make. Through regular sessions we explore the options of keeping and of placing the child. She is assisted to consider the interests of each party based on the particular facts and circumstances of that client.

This requires the client to become educated about each alternative. We use various books on pregnancy and child development to explore child-raising issues. We encourage birthmothers to babysit or observe children of different age groups. We look past the baby stage to the child at two years, four years, and thirteen years in order to fully examine the birthmother's commitment to parenthood.

We also educate our clients about the realities of adoption, including the loss/grief experience and open adoption. We encourage birthparents to attend our monthly birthparents support group, where they meet with other birthparents who are at various stages in the process, including those in the post-adoption stage (sometimes several years post-birth). This gives them an opportunity to hear about the delivery/hospital experience, the grief experience, and the reality of ongoing contact. The adoption alternative, the feelings it awakens, and the personal consequences are all explored openly to reduce the confusion and isolation for the new birthmother.

Expectant birthparents also have an opportunity to meet and talk with adoptive parents. Laura, for example, attended an adoption workshop and talked about her reasons and plans to relinquish to prospective adoptive parents. She carefully and openly articulated her love for the child, and listened carefully to the story of another birthmother who relinquished two years earlier. Laura was tearful before attending the adoption workshop because it was her twenty-second birthday and she could not celebrate with her family due to her desire to keep her pregnancy a secret. In spite of her sadness, Laura decided to attend the adoption workshop. Afterwards, she reported feeling more confident about her decision as a result of her conversation with adoptive couples. Laura also later attended a special group session where three adoptive fathers spoke of their experiences in adopting.

Decision-making is not easy for our birthmothers. They frequently are sad and often vacillate in their plans. One technique we use is to ask birthmothers to keep an ongoing journal while in counseling and to list the advantages and disadvantages of each choice.

Through intensive professional counseling, women come to terms with their pregnancy and also the decision they will make. This process is similar to the process of coping with death. Birthmothers go through stages of denial, anger, sadness, and eventually acceptance. They need to work through each stage prior to delivery. The focus of the counseling is on the future of the unborn child as well as that of the birthmother.

We have found most pregnant women want to keep their babies. Decisions, however, must be based not on "wanting" or "wishing" but on what is best for the child, as well as what is best for the birthmother. Birthmothers we have counseled who have placed their babies for adoption could have adequately parented their children as single parents. They gave up their babies only because they believed this was in the best interest of the children and themselves. Placing a child for adoption is a considered and unselfish act of love.

Barbara was eighteen years old and planning to marry the birthfather of her baby when she found out she was pregnant. His parents, however, were so upset about the pregnancy that they pressured him to break off his relationship with her. Barbara felt betrayed and alone. She considered abortion, but couldn't bring herself to keep the appointment. Barbara entered a maternity group home, still confused about her plans for the future. This was a time of intense maturation. When she decided on adoption, she was eager for her child to be raised, as she was, in a rural community. Her letter to her son demonstrates her act of love through adoption:

Dear Little One,

First of all I want to tell you I love you more than anything in this world. I don't want you to feel badly towards me because I gave you up. The reason is because I love you. I could not have supported you and given you everything I wanted you to have. I loved your father very much or so I thought. He had his own life to live and apparently you and I were not to be a part of it. I'm sure he loves you in his own way but we must have been meant to go our separate ways. You now have two parents who are very wonderful and very beautiful people who could not love you anymore than they do now. One day if you feel the need to find me for any reason I'll be here. But do not expect anything from me except love. I gave up my rights to you a long time ago and I accept that and I hope that you will also. The parents you have now are your <u>real</u> parents. They've taken care of your every need since you were only a few days old. I am the one who gave birth to you but I couldn't give you anything more, and I can give nothing now except my love. All I ask of you is to love your parents and live a good life. I pray you reach all your goals and have a happy and fulfilled life. I love you.

> May God Bless You
> and Keep You Always,
> Your Birthmother

An important task during this stage is selecting the adoptive parents. If the birthmother feels definite about adoption, she may make this decision early in her pregnancy and early in the counseling process in order to establish a close relationship with the adoptive parents during the duration of the pregnancy. In other situations, the birthmother may participate in several counseling sessions before deciding on adoption and selecting the adoptive parents.

In agency adoption the social workers typically select several couples to suggest to the birthparents. They provide the birthparents with profiles written by the social workers or letters written by the couples to enable the birthparents to make their selection. In independent adoption the birthparents typically select the adoptive parents from *all* adoptive parents available—there is no pre-selection or "screening" by third parties. Instead, that is the role and responsibility of the birthparents. In independent adoption (and some agency adoptions) prospective adoptive parents write "Birthmother Letters" in order to introduce themselves to the birthparents and to share their interest/hopes/dreams in looking forward to parenthood.

This is an example of a "Birthmother Letter" (which adoption intermediaries keep on file to show birthparents and which adoptive couples also distribute to friends and contacts in the hopes of locating a potential birthmother):

Hi,

Oh, how we have always dreamed of parenthood one day, and as yet we have not been able to
realize that dream. We dreamed of making our
child's first Halloween costume and taking them
trick-or-treating to their grandparent's house to surprise them, watching their little faces on Christmas
Day with a surprise visit from Santa Claus himself, and then our annual family reunion picnic. Coming from large Italian families, all these holidays
are happily celebrated. What has meant a lot to us
is that, between both of us, we are godparents to
8 children, which happens to be some of our best
friend's children. Larry is the best diaper changer
and Darlene enjoys going to the park and feeding
the ducks, things we long to do with a child of our
own. Reading bedtime stories, playing peek-a-boo,
holding our baby and doing a lot of kissing are part
of our dream.

For 15 years we have tried to have a family
of our own. We were advised to see an infertility
specialist as Darlene wasn't able to conceive and
she still did not get pregnant. Both our parents have
been very supportive throughout these hard times,
but they were thrilled at Thanksgiving time to find
out that we were planning to adopt. They are already
planning to buy baby clothes and toys.

Our country style home borders Mt. Diablo State
Park in the town of Danville in Northern California. Our backyard is spacious enough for swings
and jungle gyms. Our dog Andy, an all white fluffy
Lhasa Apso, loves to romp and run throughout the
yard. Living next door to a State Park has its advantages as Mother Nature is all around us: rolling
green hills to tumble down, over 100 year old oak
trees to climb, and a lot of deer.

Larry is a businessman operating a five store
retail delicatessen manufacturing and importing
business. Darlene has just resigned her position as
a Customer Relations Supervisor to devote her time

to see this adoption through and is excited about finally becoming a full time Mom.

We both love to travel, attend stage plays, symphonies, and do a lot of walking. Larry can't wait to travel to Grandma and Grandpa's cabin in the Sierra Mountains to show our child the snow for the first time. Darlene imagines a little one helping her make chocolate chip cookies (and eating all the chocolate chips), or licking the spatula and getting cake batter all over their little face with sticky fingers tugging at her apron.

If you would like to talk to us about adopting your child, please call us collect at _____ or call our Adoption Advisors at the Independent Adoption Center at (800) 877-OPEN.

In Friendship,
Larry & Darlene Cerletti

Phase Two—The Birth Experience

The second phase of an unplanned pregnancy begins with the child's birth. Although most birthmothers reach a preliminary decision before their child is born, the actual birth of their baby necessitates a reevaluation of that decision. The reality of a child evokes new emotions that must be examined. Regrettably, adoption intermediaries often encourage the birthmother, at this point, to accept the decision which she had been leaning toward without reassessing her alternatives. These intermediaries tend to focus more on the product (a child available for adoptive placement) than on the birthmother's emotional needs. Arrival of the baby, however, is a very critical stage of the unplanned pregnancy for the birthmother. If she is to accept her decision for a lifetime, post-delivery support and counseling must not be hasty or ignored.

In the hospital, we encourage the birthmother to look at her current feelings toward her baby and adoption. We also encourage all birthmothers to see, hold, and feed the child. In part, this contact with the baby reinforces the birthmother's feelings of self-worth by learning she could manage a baby if she elected to keep and parent the child. In addition, it is important for her to bond with the baby before she can separate from him—one must say "hello" before one can say "good-bye." During this time she can also explain to the baby why she has made an adoption decision.

In addition, contact with the child prevents any denial. The first stage of grieving is denial, and we want our birthmothers to move past that stage before they place the baby for adoption. We want our birthmothers to decide to place their child *only after coming to terms with that child's reality.* Crystal, a young birthmother, recalls, "I was afraid that when I saw the baby I was not going to be able to go through with the adoption, but I had to see him. I had too much curiosity. Right when I saw him I knew I couldn't keep him. I knew it would be wrong. I knew I couldn't be so selfish."

Decisions made in the post-delivery phase may be complicated by family and peer pressures. For example, we sometimes see birthgrandparents become strongly attached to their grandchild. This leads them to pressure their daughter to keep her newborn baby, usually ignoring her own desires. Intermediary support for the birthmother is once again necessary so that she may make her own decision in the face of outside pressures.

Mindy was nineteen when she discovered she was pregnant. Marriage was not a realistic alternative, so Mindy seriously considered single parenthood. She had the complete support of her parents for whatever decision she made. In fact, her parents came to visit her and the baby in the hospital and became very attached to their first grandchild. Mindy frequently fed and held her baby in the hospital and she named him Marshall. But Mindy had strong feelings about wanting her baby to have a two-parent family and she didn't feel able to handle the responsibility of single parenthood. She chose adoption and wrote the following letter to Marshall's new family:

> Dear Family,
>   Everytime I try to start this letter I get stuck. I really don't know what to say to you. I know you will be good parents and take good care of my son

and love him as your very own. That makes me feel good and very happy. My parents are also glad to know he will be well taken care of. My mother loved him very much because he was her first grandchild. It was very hard for her as well as for me to give him up. He is a very special little boy to us.

I will ask a few things of you. Please help guide him toward what he would like to be but please don't pressure him. And please let him know about me and help him to understand that I didn't give him up because I didn't want him or because something was wrong with him.

I would definitely like to meet him and your family someday. I will in no way try to win him back. I just want to let him know in person that I love him.

Your Son's Birthmother

In some states, legal relinquishment papers may be signed by birthmothers ready for that decision while still in the hospital. In other states, the relinquishment/consent is signed at some later date (typically the time period is dictated by state laws).

In all cases, we recommend that the baby be placed directly from the hospital with the adopting parents, rather than utilizing foster care. This means that in cases where the birthparents have not yet signed the consent, the adoptive parents must be willing to take some legal risk. This enables the adoptive family and baby to bond with one another from the beginning, and it also minimizes the separations and adjustments for the infant.

Phase Three—Living with the Adoption Decision

The final phase of the unplanned pregnancy begins for the birthmother after the child is placed in the adoptive home. The post-birth period is the time the birthmother both grieves and begins the process of accepting her decision. We now understand that counseling at this stage is essentially grief counseling. One birthmother who placed her child for adoption ten years ago recalls that her agency provided no post-placement guidance. She relates painfully, "No one told me that I would experience overpowering feelings of grief. I was totally unprepared for the emotions that hit me." This same birthmother also lacked understanding family members or friends to assist her through the painful days and nights of missing her child. The professional intermediaries who should have been with her were either rationalizing that she did not care about her birthchild (first myth of adoption) or that she had forgotten by now (third myth).

In contrast, we acknowledge the feelings of grief felt by birthparents by preparing them prior to delivery and by providing post-placement grief counseling. Counseling begins on the day of the child's adoptive placement (typically at discharge from the hospital), which marks the start of the child's existence separate from his birthmother. Our involvement then continues as long as the birthparent feels our support is necessary.

Since our birthmothers select the adoptive parents of their child, they feel a special love for the adoptive parents. They know that placement day is a day of joy for the people they picked to parent their child. This helps ease some of their own sadness. In fact, birthparents with open adoptions work through the normal feelings of loss and grief much more quickly and easily because they have selected the parents for their baby, have met with them, and will continue to have contact with them over the years. This gives them a peace of mind not found in closed adoption and enables them to more easily deal with their grief.

Letters, pictures, and gifts are frequently exchanged between birthparents and adoptive parents during the post-birth period (and, in open adoptions, there are also visits). Hal and Marcie, an adoptive couple, wrote two letters to the birthmother of their son. The first was written one month after placement and the second one seven months later. Both were eagerly received by a birthmother working to integrate and accept her act of placing a child:

To our son's biological mother,

It is impossible to describe the joy of being presented with such a beautiful child. We had wanted a child for a long time and had tried very hard to have our own. Now we are sure that adopting your biological son was what God meant for us. He has brought us so much happiness—we could never have asked for a more perfect child.

When we went to pick him up that day, we were nervous wondering what he would look like and how we would feel about him. But when we saw him, all the nervousness went away. He was more that we had ever imagined. We have loved him from that moment, and every day we can feel the love grow.

We feel, as you do, that he deserves every chance to enjoy life. Being good parents to him is very important to us, and we promise to do everything we can to help him have a happy and fulfilling life. We will help him to develop and grow and give him every opportunity to get the most possible out of life.

We want you to know that you are very special to us, too. We know that releasing your child was difficult, and we want to assure you that he will always be very much loved by us. We wish you the best, and while we know you will never forget your biological son, we hope that when you think of him it will be with happiness and good feelings. That is also how we want him to feel about you. It's so little for us just to say thanks—but thank you very much. God bless you always, and may He give you all the love and happiness the world has to offer.

Love,
Your biological son's parents

To our son's birthmother,

Hi! I heard from our social worker today, and she said you would like to have a picture of the baby. We are sending one when he was about five months old; we hope you like it.

We think about you a lot and hope everything is going okay for you. We are all doing really fine and are enjoying our new little family member so much.

He's eight months old now—it's hard to believe he's been with us that long. He's still a very happy and content little boy. He has been healthy and made it through the winter without anything serious. He has five teeth and is starting to eat some table foods which he loves. He's also learning to drink from a cup. He has been crawling for about a month and can pull himself to a standing position and walk along a sofa or table by himself. I think he will walk for sure within a month. He does "pat-a-cakes" when we say the words for him and has also started making some really silly noises with his hand in his mouth. He likes to pull hair, including his own, which still looks like it's going to be blond. He has beautiful blue eyes and the sweetest little smile. He loves people—we think it's really nice because he's not shy or afraid of other people. He gets all excited when he's around other babies especially. I think he's going to be very outgoing and friendly. He still loves his bath. When he gets in the tub he swims and splashes and squeals with excitement. We can't wait until it gets warmer so we can get him a little splash pool to play in. He also has a puppy that he likes. The puppy usually stays outside, so he crawls over to the window to visit with it. When we put him outside in his swing sometimes, the puppy licks his toes, and they both think that's funny. He's still very curious and observant. We never have trouble if we take him anywhere (to the grocery store, mall, restaurant, etc.) because he's so busy looking at everything that he doesn't get fussy.

So we are really happy with the way everything has worked out. We hope to be able to adopt

another baby in a couple of years. I think I told
you before how sad and depressed I used to be when
I kept trying and trying and could never get pregnant. I used to pray and wonder why it could happen to other people and not me. Since we have had
this baby with us, I have never again wondered
why I never got pregnant. There is no doubt in my
mind that God, in His way, was saving us to be
the parents of this wonderful little boy. I hope you
feel as good about it as we do.

Please take care of yourself, and God be with
you always. I love you and feel close to you even
though I really don't know you And please feel
assured that your biological son is very much loved
and cared for.

Love,
Your birthson's mother

Sylvia, the birthmother who received these letters, told
us, "When I think of him, I think of him being with his puppy
dog or in the bath. I just think of him as being happy." She
adds, "In a way I was a chosen person to have this baby
for someone else who couldn't." Today she describes adoption as "giving love all the way around."

At this early post-placement phase, correspondence
and pictures of the baby from the adoptive parents assure
the birthmother that her child is developing and happy. In
turn, the birthmother can assure the adoptive parents of their
place in the child's life. Polly, an eighteen-year-old birthmother, wrote the following letter to her daughter's parents
shortly after the placement:

Dear Adoptive Parents,

I hope you are enjoying your daughter. I know
she will be happy there with you, and I hope you
love her as much as I do. I'm glad she has a loving
family such as yours. It gives me a great feeling
of security to know she has parents like you and
a big brother.

I can imagine how much you have wanted this

child, and I thank you so much for giving her what
I could not. I can not begin to express my feelings
of gratitude.

   I hope everything is going well at your home,
and I wish you the best always.

                    Take care,
                    Polly

The post-birth stage also involves "reentering the
world" and establishing new relationships. The birthmother
must decide "whom do I tell," and how to respond if someone says, "How could you do that?" Birthmothers often
worry about dating again and some must come to terms with
anger directed at males in general. In addition, family adjustments can be awkward since families tend to deny that the
pregnancy occurred.

   To deal with these post-adoption issues, we provide
both individual counseling and a monthly birthparents support group. The group consists of other birthmothers who
have placed their children for adoption and are in the
process of both accepting their decisions and rebuilding
their lives. Discussions center on such topics as sex, birth
control, family interaction, assertiveness training, and ongoing contact with the adoptive parents and child. Often our
birthmothers feel "no one else fully understands," and the
group becomes their opportunity to talk about the child and
themselves. Attendance is usually regular during the first few
months and then sporadic. The group provides essential
social support and information necessary to get through this
final phase of the unplanned pregnancy. Each birthmother
progresses through the stages of grief at her own pace.

   Sandra, age nineteen, attended our support group sessions regularly for an entire year. It took Sandra that much
time before she was finally able to say goodbye in this letter:

Dear Daughter,
   I am writing this letter almost one year after
I had you because I feel like it is something that
I must do before too long. I want you to know my
reasons for giving you up and tell you that you are

now and will be forever in my thoughts. There were many times that I would change my mind but in the end my decision was the best for everyone all the way around. I want you to know that if your birthfather and I could have provided for you everything necessary, we would have done so. When I say provided for you, I mean everything needed to raise a child including love for each other, which was not there. I don't think I was old enough to take the responsibility of raising a child either. I am sure that if your birthfather and I loved each other as much as we love you we could have done it. However, it wasn't that way between us. We thought we did, but when it came to talking about the rest of our lives, I really don't think it was there. I am sure now that you are happy and have the most wonderful parents ever dreamed of They are warm, loving people and I admire them very much. I know you will grow into a beautiful person and have a great life. I cannot put down into writing the way I feel about you. Now that a year has passed by, my life has gone on and the memories that I have of you are stored in a special place in my heart. Your birthfather and I have remained friends and we both hope that we may see you someday. I hope your feelings will be the same and you can understand our reasons for placing you for adoption.

Love always,
Your Birthmother

P.S. I also want you to know that you were the biggest baby in the hospital nursery and surely the healthiest. Good luck always.

DECIDING ABOUT FUTURE CONTACT

In agency adoption, the birthmother typically makes one final decision before she terminates her relationship with the agency. She must answer the question: "Do you want future contact from your child?'' The birthmother signs a document about whether she wants records opened if her child later (at age 18 or older) decides to search. In our experience, 99% of birthmothers consent to future contact. In some agencies, birthmothers also are invited to participate in exchanging ongoing correspondence and current pictures with their adoptive parents, but typically the agency remains the intermediary for this contact. Most birthmothers are positive about both opportunities.

In open, independent adoption, birthparents and adoptive parents share full identifying information from the beginning and have access to direct ongoing contact over the years. The "open records at age 18" issue is not relevant, because these individuals remain in contact over the years, and the adoptive parents can easily put the adopted child/adult in direct contact with his birthmother.

Each birthparent ends her relationship with the adoption intermediary when she is ready, and always with the assurance that she may contact us for information or assistance at any future time. We know her decision was a lifetime one; therefore, we plan to meet her needs as time and the healing process demand, even if it takes that lifetime.

Ultimately we find that our parents—both birth and adoptive—provide most of the long-term support for each other. Any communication is usually welcomed by all parties. Pam, the birthmother who wrote the following letter, thought she had lost this special relationship when she stopped hearing from Raymond and Debbie, the adoptive parents of her daughter. The adoptive parents had written but their letter had disappeared somehow in the mail:

> Dear Raymond and Debbie,
>   I was so relieved to hear from the agency that I just couldn't wait to write you a letter. The reason I haven't written is because I felt that it would be in vain. The last letters I wrote were in the beginning of February. I got no response and I was very worried and upset. I thought you folks just didn't want to write, so I've left you alone. It's good to know that you do want to hear from me.

Things have changed quite a bit for me! I've got a job at a bank downtown here as a teller. It's a good job except for the pay. In November the bank financed a car for me. It's real nice! It's a little Plymouth Arrow. I haven't got my own place yet, but I'm working on it. It won't be long. Best of all, I have a boyfriend who I love very much. He's a good person. One thing I know is that he loves children. I've told him about Brenda and all of you. He thinks it's wonderful to have adoptive parents who care enough to try to keep in touch. I do too. If possible, it would be nice to have some more pictures of Brenda. I'm dying to know how she's doing and what's going on in her life. I'm sure she's just as beautiful as I imagine. I enclosed a picture of myself. I don't look very happy 'cause the sun was in my eyes. I'll have to send a better one when I have them done in a portrait studio. That's me, anyway (pudgy). I only want to say one thing about her birthfather. He cares more about Brenda than he does about himself. That's enough about me, except that I hope to have another child whose as beautiful as Brenda. I can't wait to find out what's going on there with all of you (including Brad). I'd love to hear from you.

Joyfully,
Pam

Pam's letter is "joyous" because she is allowed open communication to people who have a permanent place in her thoughts. The depth of the bond that can form between our "collective parents" is truly unique. The next letter, written by Dawn two years after her son's adoptive placement, reveals just how and why the bond is so special:

Dearest Terry, Nancy, and Drew,

Thank you so very much for those wonderful pictures. Drew is such a beautiful boy. I am so proud of him. I have been keeping all of Drew's pictures in my photo-album with the exception of two that

I carry with me. Since you sent a picture of you both, I now added those pictures to my album. As I was putting the pictures in the photo book, I thought to myself "now I have my family all together," and that is how I feel. You are a very special and important part of my life. You, Terry and Nancy, have a special place in my heart. Drew holds a special (very special) spot all his own, and no one but no one will ever take that love for you three away from me. I just want you to know that I have a big, big heart that holds lots, lots of love. So much love that I will never be able to express all the love I have for Drew and the both of you. I do know one thing, that love grows and grows each day. More and more as I look at Drew's pictures and more and more as I read your letters. I hope and pray that we will be able to continue writing and exchanging pictures. I also was curious and excited when I received your pictures. Nancy, you have very pretty eyes and such a kind friendly smile. Terry you're very handsome. I know you are tall, but boy, you have large hands. I bet you'd make a good football player or basketball, too.

I don't think I would feel the same toward you two, if it wasn't for your letters. Knowing and being showed that you do care for me and you really, really do care and love our son Drew, has lifted a heavy load off my shoulders.

Sure, I wish I would of had a good home for our son and a father, cause I would never of put Drew up for adoption. But that was just it—I didn't have the surroundings and environment to bring up a child. I feel that it would of been selfish to of tried to raise Drew by myself. At the time I was all alone. It was just me. I used to cry and cry before Drew was born. What was I to do! Oh, I tell you I lived in a nightmare. I tried to hide the fact that I was pregnant from my friends and family. (My good old boyfriend left me.) It was just me and Drew. I had no one to turn to, talk to. I used to sit down and tell all my problems to a big white stuffed rabbit I have. That old rabbit knows me better than anyone.

Then I thought to myself, my baby (at that time, now he's ours) is going to have the best, and that's when I made up my mind to relinquish my baby. It was at that moment I hurt. I didn't know where Drew would go, who would be raising him. I had all these questions, these thoughts running through my head, one after another. When Drew was born (which was the greatest experience in my life) and they hit me with those papers (adoption relinquishment papers) I felt confused and hurt, my life was gone, down the drain. It wasn't until I received three pictures of Drew and a letter from my social worker that I felt a little less guilt. Then when I received your letter that was handwritten by you to me, that the guilt, the sorrow, the confusion went away. I knew Drew was where he belonged and belongs. You know that saying, time heals all—well it heals, but the past—at least for me—will always be remembered. I was also told the old saying "Out of sight, out of mind"—not so. I think about Drew and you both all the time.

I wonder at times what it would be like to give Drew a hug and kiss, to hold him, to play with him, but then I realize that you do that for me. I wouldn't want Drew with any other parents. You are the best. I can tell by all of Drew's pictures he is so happy and healthy looking.

I wish for a day where I'll be able to come to you, Terry and Nancy, and tell you how much I love you and all the gratitude I have for you. I wish for a day where I'll be able to confront Drew about our situation. I hope Drew and I will someday meet and become friends. I know I will never be his mother. I don't want that. You are the only parents that he'll grow to love and know. But I want to be able to talk to my family face to face because there is so much love and feelings toward you that

I just can't put down on paper. I know God created
Drew through me for you, but God also created you
for Drew and me!

It made me feel so good when you said Drew
looks like me. I agree. My mother and I got out some
baby pictures of me and compared them with Drew's.
We came to the conclusion Drew has my nose, my
smile, hair and shape of face. He got his big blue
eyes from his father—Sam as I think I mentioned
in a previous letter. . . .

I have 4 months of school left until I graduate.
I am really excited about my career and future. I'm
looking forward to getting settled into a job. Most
of all I'm looking forward to getting married in July
or August, and within 3 years (give or take a year),
starting a family of my own. I know God will let
Jim and I know when that time will be. God sure
blessed us with a beautiful son, Drew, and God
blessed Drew with you.

> God Bless You and Keep You,
> All My Love
> Dawn

Dawn's letter is open and secure. She can write of her
pain and of her hopes for her future to the adoptive parents
of her son. Her healthy adjustment is the result of careful
professional counseling. The task is not simple— adoption
intermediaries must commit time, personnel, and other
resources necessary. But to do less would be a disservice
to those birthparents who select adoption as their best
alternative.

8
Adoption—
A New Definition

Legacy of an Adopted Child

Once there were two women
Who never knew each other
One you do not remember
The other you call mother

Two different lives shaped to make yours one
One became your guiding star
The other became your sun

The first gave you life
And the second taught you to live in it
The first gave you a need for love
And the second was there to give it

One gave you a nationality
The other gave you a name
One gave you the seed of talent
The other gave you an aim

One gave you emotions
The other calmed your fears
One saw your first sweet smile
The other dried your tears

One gave you up—it was all that she could do.
The other prayed for a child.
And God led her straight to you.

And now you ask me through your tears,
The age old questions through the years;

Heredity or Environment—which are you
the product of:

Neither my darling—neither
  Just two different kinds of love.
                    Anonymous

We have identified the myths of adoption and explored how new adoption practices affect adoptive parents and birthparents. In this chapter, we propose a new definition of adoption. This definition is offered primarily for the last member of the adoption drama—the adoptee.

Our definition of adoption is a simple statement, but contains no simple concepts:

Adoption is the process of accepting the responsibility of raising an individual who has two sets of parents.

To understand what this definition conveys we will examine first what we term the grammar of adoption and then the precise words of two phrases within our definition. Why the emphasis on "responsibility?" What are the consequences of the ending phrase "an individual who has two sets of parents?"

THE GRAMMAR OF ADOPTION

We began our definition with the phrase "adoption is the process." When couples elect to adopt, they think and talk in terms of adoption being the process necessary to form their family. Emphasis is on the act or event of adoption. Such statements as the following are typical: "We have started the adoption process," or "The agency will place a child with us next week." In a sense, adoption is being used here to describe a single event which will form their family.

In contrast, once the couple does adopt a child, a semantic problem develops. Parents who want to share with another that their child was adopted stumble with such statements as: "Betsy is my adopted daughter"; "I have two special children and one natural child"; "I have one chosen child and one of my own''; or ''I only have one biological child.'' In each instance, the terms they use to convey an ''adoptive status'' are applied as adjectives to describe the child. The dictionary defines an adjective as ''denoting a quality of the thing named.'' By applying ''adopted'' or ''special'' or ''chosen'' or ''biological'' to the child, it sounds as if there are different kinds of children (as represented by adjectives) instead of different ways for children to enter a family (as represented by a process).

Adoption is a process. We advocate that the process be kept distinct from the person who is the adoptee. On the simplest level this means preferring ''Betsy was adopted'' to ''Betsy is an adopted child.'' The first (Betsy was adopted) correctly describes a single and past event in her life. This is no different from a birthmother proud of the experience of giving birth describing to another, ''I had my son by cesarean birth.'' The same birthmother would not refer to that child after the event as ''my cesarean son.''

By contrast, ''Betsy is an adopted child'' or even ''Betsy is special because she is adopted'' conveys an ongoing significance to the state of being adopted. This is potentially dangerous because of the subtle implication that adopted children are somehow different from natural children who do not have labels attached to them. In addition, if Betsy is described as ''special'' or ''chosen,'' that means someone is less special or valuable as a person. If Betsy is not a ''natural child'' that makes her ''unnatural'' or at least not normal. Do these labels all mean that at one point Betsy was not so special because she was not wanted?

The goal of our definition is more than a careful selection of the ''right word.'' Being clear that adoption is a process recognizes that there are different ways to create a family, but the children of that family are not different. When speaking in terms of the way the family was formed, the preferable approach is, ''Betsy was adopted.'' When talking about Betsy herself, she is simply ''our daughter.'' Emphasis remains where it belongs.

Frank and Ellen, an adoptive couple who waited for several years for their son, enjoy describing their adoption experience and do so with pride. Note that when they want to talk about the adoption they use such phrases as, "manner he entered our family." When they speak of their son, the terminology is simply "our precious little son," without qualifying adjectives:

To the Birth-Mother of Our Son:

Somehow writing this letter is much harder than we could have ever anticipated. There are so many feelings inside of us it's really difficult to put them down on paper. There are no words to tell you how grateful we are to be the proud new parents of a darling little son. He is definitely God's gift to us in life. It's positively a dream come true. One day we were just an ordinary couple who had wanted children for many years and then suddenly we are blessed with one of God's most dearest gifts— a baby boy! There is nothing on this earth more precious to us than our little son!

In the future we will be impressing upon him the importance of life and a close family relationship. We don't feel that the manner in which he entered our family is of any importance at all. The important thing is that he's ours for keeps now and that's what really counts.

Please know that we will tell him everything we know about where he came from. We want him to grow up knowing his natural parents did what was best for him at the time. We hope he will think of the whole situation with understanding and compassion. It sincerely touches our hearts to know that some women care enough about their child to give him up knowing he will be placed in a loving, happy home.

We believe that it is God's will that we can't have children naturally. But we now know that God has a plan for each of us and for months when we were sure he'd forgotten about us and we'd even doubted him, he came through and showed us that he had other more important plans for us. Now our lives have taken on a whole new meaning.

We know this must be a very difficult time for you. We think about you many times during the course of a week. We wonder how you have adjusted and if you will ever want him to look you up. We were told that you were also adopted. This being the case we hope you will want to share any information you may obtain about your natural parents so that he will be able to have answers to his many questions.

We want to help our son to obtain any goal he should set for himself. If he should decide that he'd like to meet you some day—well, we're all for it. That is, of course, if it is also what you want. We would not want to invade your privacy or interrupt your life in any way unless you say it is alright.

We do not feel threatened by you nor do we feel like his meeting you will change the way we feel about each other. We love each other very much and we will have been with him through good times and bad and so whatever he decides is also our decision.

Our hearts will always hold a special place for you and we will pray that God will give you the strength to accept what has happened to you and know that someday you will realize that you made the right decision and find out what God's plans for your life will be. Sometimes when you least expect it, there comes a miracle from God to set your life back on track.

Many thanks to you! We know that what you did was only for yourself and the love of a little one but that decision has affected our lives greatly too.

May God Bless You and Keep You Forever and Ever and may we say "Thank You" for allowing this little boy to come into the world and bless our lives.

Gratefully yours,
Baby's New Parents

Adoptive parents often tend initially to glamorize adoption with the terms "special" or "chosen" in order to convey the experiences and emotion they have invested in the process. Their initial tendency is also a protective counter to bolster their status, in case others equate an infrequently used process to a second best one. The definition we promote assists our parents to recognize that the process of giving birth and the process of adoption result in the same objective—a family. Once that family is formed the procedure is over and should become a fact in the family's life history, as any other past event. Although the act of adopting is not the most frequent way Americans form their families, the relationship so formed is just as complete. Again, distinguishing the procedure from the family so formed prevents subtle messages or thoughts that the family is less valuable or second best to the family formed through the birth process.

ACCEPTING RESPONSIBILITY

Adoption is the process of **accepting the responsibility** of raising an individual who has two sets of parents.

When adoptive parents accept a child into their family they acquire some unique parental obligations. Adoptive parents are accountable for telling their child he was adopted, and for sharing adoption information in a natural and honest manner. This allows the adoptee to integrate simple and straightforward facts into his evolving identity.

We still hear that in some cases adoptive parents have waited to share the fact of their child's adoption until the child "could understand." This approach anticipates a "right time," but contains many hazards. The most dramatic danger, of course, is when the "right time" does not occur when the child could first understand, because the adoptive parents keep "forgetting." Finally, the adoptee is told, possibly at the same time he is coping with the identity-seeking teen years. The shock of such a revelation at this time can be very destructive. The adoptee can understandably react as if his entire life has been a lie. He may even believe that he no longer has a foundation upon which to base his value system. Trust in the family unit can be forever shattered. Although this scenario still occurs, such a blow to the adoptee's identity and security is unnecessary.

More subtle hazards of waiting to share adoption information until the adoptee can understand include overemphasizing the significance of his adoption. Waiting usually means that the telling includes an elaborately staged family conference called to convey an important message. This creates an atmosphere that says adoption is so different we treat the subject (and you?) as out of the ordinary.

Another danger of waiting until the "right time" is that the unveiling occurs at a period in time when the adoptee is not interested. Because he does not ask questions and shows no other interest at this initial family session, his parents assume he both understands and is satisfied with the information they did share. Parents might even be tempted to seek the solace of this rationalized conclusion because of their own need not to remember or talk about his adoption. Often these parents are surprised and saddened by future probing questions from the same adoptee. Their answers at this point reflect these feelings of surprise, sadness, and some anger. Adoptees quickly pick up on their parents' feelings. Recently Adam, an adult adoptee speaking at a group meeting remembered, "For every question I was able to ask my parents, I had a thousand more." He never asked those additional questions because he was sensitive to the distress the inquiry would cause his parents.

To counter these hazards, we advocate a gradual and natural approach that keeps the responsibility always on the adoptive parents. We refer to our method as a building block process and it begins when the child is an infant (assuming an early placement). We advocate this early approach because of the fact that children learn to talk by imitating words they hear. If they hear "adoption" in the home, they will learn to use the word even before they fully understand its meaning. Many of our two-year-olds tell people, "I 'dopted" with the same understanding as when they hold up two fingers in response to questions of age. As adults, these adoptees will not recall their first introduction to adoption. The term and the subject will be naturally accepted. To assure the adoptee this type of introduction, adoptive parents have the responsibility of using the word "adoption" freely in the home during their family's initial bonding period. This is difficult for parents to do during the early adoptive period because many work to deny the realities of adoption. To safeguard the adoptee's future attitudes toward himself, adoption, and his parents, we strongly recommend that this first building block be provided.

Between two and five years of age, the child's next building block is offered by the adoptive parents. The objective is for the adoptee to associate the word adoption with the formation of his family. A second goal is to accomplish this familiarization in a relaxed manner aimed at his level of understanding. This can be done by reading or telling the adoptee stories of adoption. Homemade picture scrapbooks of the child or such books as Carole Livingston's *Why Was I Adopted?* (1978) work very well. Such a presentation, combined with the previous free use of the word, lays a foundation for the adoptee to accept his adoption in much the same way he accepts his eye or hair color. That is, no value judgments are placed on the adoption process. He sees it as neither good nor bad.

Remember adoption is a process—a process that does not describe the adoptee as an individual. That concept, however, would be difficult to explain to a four-year-old. Therefore, the manner we convey adoption facts should be calculated to nonverbally express our attitude. We recommend a storybook approach because the preschooler loves books. We also find the storybook setting creates an informal atmosphere while giving adoptive parents the instructional support of visual aides.

Subsequent building blocks are added as the curiosity of the child and ingenuity of the parents dictate. School age children begin to ask in-depth questions about their heritage and about the two individuals who are their birthparents. This begins the period when adoptive parents must deal with their own feelings in response to the adoptee's questions. This is especially true when the child uses such phrases as "my other mother" or "my real father." Although we acknowledge their own emotional needs, adoptive parents have the crucial task during these years of keeping communication channels open. Their objective is to create a comfortable atmosphere that says, "your questions are welcomed and will be answered."

In order to convey honest facts to the adoptee, adoptive parents must know and understand birthparents. This includes fully exploring the myths of adoption and their own particular stereotypes. We assist our adoptive parents with this exploration and with their own emotional growth. We are convinced adoptive parents can comfortably share accurate adoption information once they have resolved any ambivalence toward their child's birthparents.

The following letter was written by an adoptive mother to the birthmother of her son more than three years after the adoption. The letter reflects security in her own role and in the role the birthmother plays in Cliff's life. They will be able to communicate with their son about his birthparents without sadness, envy, or threat. We know Cliff is only one of the several beneficiaries:

Dear Dee,

We have read your letters and looked at your pictures so many times. I'm sorry that it has taken me so long to write, but it's been hard to think of what to say.

We have appreciated, cherished and saved your letters and poems for Cliff. I know they will be very important to him to know how much you care and your feelings. Your letters have helped reassure us, and eased our fears.

Cliff is the light in our lives. He is growing so much everyday. It's amazing how quickly he changes. I'm enclosing a recent picture. He looks like he has your coloring, and your pictures will mean so much to him.

It really sounds like school and your job have kept you busy. I hope your music is recorded, too. My brother is very musical. He writes and plays his own music as a hobby.

We have gotten brave and are trying to adopt another baby. We are waiting and when we ask Cliff what he wants he says "I want a BIG baby!"

Thank you for your letters and thoughtfulness. I hope things continue to go well for you, because you are someone who has an important place in our hearts.

Yours Truly,
Jill and Mike

As the child matures, further additional details of his adoption will unfold. During this time, adoptive parents must carefully balance the desire to allow the adoptee to explore the topic at his own pace against the peril of the subject becoming a closed one in the home. An unhealthy closure might easily occur if adoptive parents assume that silence means no interest. Adoptees tell us a different story. Again, we emphasize that adoptive parents (not the child) have the responsibility to periodically bring up the subject. This is done either to explore possible areas of concerns or to merely reassure the adoptee that the subject is not taboo.

These responsibilities are unique. Adoptive parents provide more than the moral, legal, and nurturing aspects of parenthood. They prepare their child to face life with an open, informed, and relaxed acceptance of the fact that he was adopted. Such responsibility might appear awesome but our adoptive parents, like the following adoptive father, gladly accept the task:

Dear Friend,

I'm sorry I have not written to you before now. You have been on my mind many times since my wife and I received your baby daughter into our home. Our new daugher is very precious to us. She has been a joy to watch as she learns to do something new every day. She now rolls over both ways and is beginning to hold her bottle by herself. She likes to chew on her hands but she doesn't suck her thumb. We have been lucky none of our children have been thumb suckers.

Your/our daughter has been very healthy. She weighs 17 pounds at the present time. She is a beautiful child with a fantastic disposition. She sleeps all night without waking usually. Occasionally she wakes up at night but all she does is giggle herself back to sleep.

Thank you for allowing me to be her adoptive father. I promise you that I will give her all the love I have to give. She will be raised as a Christian in a Christian home. I will do everything I can to prepare her for a complex world. She will be made aware of who she is, and we will do all we can to help her become a whole and complete person. We love her more than you can imagine.

We pray for you constantly. Please don't worry about her. She is happy, well, and loved very dearly.

God Bless You
Your child's Adoptive Father

TWO SETS OF PARENTS

Adoption is the process of accepting
the responsibility of raising an
**individual who has two sets
of parents.**

The final aspect of our definition of adoption emphasizes that adoptive parents do not own the adoptee. Whether we give birth to our children or adopt them, children are individuals and not our possessions to forever hold close. We emphasize this primarily as a reminder because adoptive parents tend to protect and cling to the child they struggled so long to find.

All parents experience some anxiety as their child matures and approaches the age when he will leave home. Physical separation, however, is only one aspect of the anxiety adoptive parents feel. At some point, adoptive parents may have to cope with the additional fear of an emotional separation from their child—more specifically, they fear that their child will eventually reject them in favor of those "other parents." We often hear this fear phrased, "If my child searches for her birthparents, I will have been nothing more than a babysitter all these years" (fourth myth revisited). A more subtle expression of the same fear is, "If I have a good relationship with my daughter, she will still love me if she finds her birthmother."

Both statements reflect a belief that adoptive parents always risk losing their child. No matter how much they may wish away this fear, adoptive parents can not change the existence of another set of parents for their child. Love for a child is a commitment to raise the child, not to cut that child off from the people who partly represent his past and his future.

We cannot say if the adoptee will have disturbing questions about the individuals who gave him life, his physical appearance, and inherited potential. We do not know if the adoptee will need to search for his heritage and touch a piece of that reality. We are convinced, however, that we can prepare our adoptive parents for these possibilities. This preparation includes examining the origin of the adoptive parents' apprehensions. For some adoptive parents, their fears stem from the second-best feelings left in the aftermath of their infertility or sudden confrontation with the realities of adoption. Certainly a parent has a more difficult time sustaining an "as if she were my daughter" pretense when that daughter is actively searching for "other parents."

Once we examine the emotions involved, we find that parents can provide their children honest answers and assistance without a sense of failure. By facing their own fright of emotional separation, our parents can better accept their child's need to have a whole identity. Of course that means knowing the people who gave her life. The following excerpt from a letter written by an adoptive mother to her daughter's birthmother illustrates our point:

> ... Shannon, you don't have to worry about Leslie knowing you love her. We know what a sacrifice you've made and we intend to tell her how much you loved and cared for her. I'll see that she gets your letter, pictures, and the lovely blanket. We won't have to compete for her love. I'm sure she'll hold

a special spot for each of us. We love you for the
life you've given us and we'll see that Leslie shares
our feelings.

I don't have a picture to send now. I want to
send one of her smiling. I will try to send you one
soon.

We hope your adjustment will go as easy as
Leslie's has. I think of you often as I hold my very
special and very wonderful daughter.

Julie

It is quite normal for children to want to know about their
heritage. No matter how much love adoptive parents give
their children, a certain curiosity remains. That curiosity has
nothing to do with the child's love for the adoptive parents.
We are convinced that when adoptees do find their birthparents, the result usually relieves everyone. After the mystery
is solved, the adoptee is freed to move on with his own life,
and his adoptive parents finally learn they will not be
rejected. Feelings of frustration and doubt are erased.

Consider, for example, how the adoptee and parents
might feel after meeting Stephanie, the sensitive birthmother
who wrote the following two letters:

My Dearest Tara,

I'm writing this letter to you so I can tell you
about me and also explain my reasons for not keeping you. First, a little bit of my history. I gave birth
to you at the age of 19. You are the best thing that
ever happened to me. I have lots of hobbies. They
are swimming, horseback riding, reading myster-
ies, and snow/water skiing. Enough of that. I need
to tell you my reasons now. Please don't think that
I don't love you because I didn't keep you. I didn't
keep you, well it's hard to explain. But I will try
anyway. I need to set it straight. I was young to
have a child but I still wanted to go through with
it. Also, your father and I weren't ready for marriage and a baby at the same time. They are very
big responsibilities. I wanted very much to keep you

and to raise you myself but you needed both a mom and a dad who already have a home and will see that you get a good education, and lots and lots of love between the parents and for you and your brother.

I do love you very, very much. I have so much love for you that you just can't describe it in words. You are always in my prayers and thoughts every-day. I know they're taking real good care of you and also God is watching out for you too. Fortunately, I was able to get to see you till you were 3 weeks old. Your were such a good baby. You weighed 11 lbs and 4 oz. and were 22 1/2 in. long. Also you came 2 weeks late. But I didn't mind, it was well worth it. You are such a joy to me. I'm just sorry I wasn't able to raise you When I get married I know I'll have more children but you were my first and are the most precious of all. I will never forget you. When you're old enough and you would like to find me, that would make me very happy, if that is what you want to do. Giving you up was the most hardest decision that I ever had to make. But Tara, I was only thinking of your future and welfare. May happiness always come your way. I wish you all the luck in the world. Always remember I love you very much. I know you'll be very happy with your family. They love you very much too. Look up to your big brother. I'm sure he'll give you good advice as you get older.

I Love You,
Your mom, Stephanie

Dear Parents,

I am now getting around to writing ya'lls let-ter. It's not that I have been putting it off or any-thing, its just that this is not an easy thing for me to do. In fact, writing this letter to ya'll is very important to me. It really means an awful lot to me. When I was 3 months pregnant and I knew Tara's father wouldn't be getting married, I then realized adoption was the best positive step that I could have made for my baby and myself. I didn't know a lot about adoption but I sure know a lot more now than I did at first. I know in my heart that I made the right decision and I'm awfully glad that you and your husband are happy with your new addition to the family.

Ya'lls autobiographies were nice and thats why I selected you to be the parents of my baby. I'm sure you know that I wanted to keep her but she does need a mom and dad. Besides, on my salary right now I wouldn't be able to give a whole lot to her except lots of love and care. I think that is most important. My social worker has told me what a good baby she is. She was that way in the hospital too. I'm very proud of her. She is my pride and joy, even though I won't get to see her grow up into a grown woman. She'll always be very precious to me. I love her very much and I would like for ya'll to know that. When you do start to tell Tara she is adopted and if she ask questions about me please remember I love her and that I was thinking of her future. I do not want her growing up thinking I don't love her. . . .

During labor with Tara wasn't too hard. Every now and then the pain was just a little unbearable. But after 17 1/2 hours she finally came. That was the proudest moment in my life. God really helped me select a good set of parents. Thank you for wanting her and for loving her enough to adopt another child. Ya'll are very special people to me. Pat and Betty [two adoptive mothers] were with me during labor and that made it a lot easier for me when it got really rough. Betty even got to see her head crown. That's something Betty has never been able to experience and so it was special to her and to me. I spent a month at the maternity home but I did not enjoy it all that much but I'm thankful that there is a place that we could go to when we didn't have any other.

Do you think it would be alright to get another picture of Tara please? I enjoy looking at her pictures and looking back on the times I was able to spend with her. It does not depress me. So please don't think that. To tell you the truth, it helps me get through the day when I think of her or even talk about her with my friends. I am giving you 2 pictures that were taken down at the agency office. I would like for Tara to have them please. Well I guess I've written all I can for right now. Another thing, ongoing correspondence will be just fine with me. My thought and prayers are with you. May God be with you always.

Stephanie

In total, our definition of adoption implicitly declares the adoptee as our primary client, while emphasizing the equal role of his two sets of parents. Each parent has contributed to the person the adoptee is or will become. The interaction among these three parties has been referred to as an adoption triangle. Although a triangle best indicates the three-sided relationship, we would add to this concept. We would place the adoptee at the apex of the triangle to signify the fact he brought the triangle together, and correctly focus our attention on his needs. His parents we would place on an equal level below, one set not displacing the other. The result is a picture of five people fate has tied together.

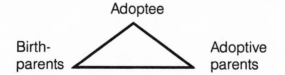

Adoptee

Birth-parents   Adoptive parents

As previously detailed, each individual in our triangle experiences separate losses and unique pains. Adoptive parents experience the grief caused by their infertility and consequential sadness because they cannot be "total" parents. Birthparents sustain the dramatic loss of the parental role of nurturing and shaping their child. Finally, the adoptee loses because he will never know what it is like to totally belong to only one mother and one father. To deny the invisible ties of emotion that bond them together would be to live a lie.

Three final letters in this chapter are offered to illustrate just how strong these ties of emotion can be for the individuals daily involved in the adoption drama. The first letter was written by an adoptive mother who has accepted the fact that adoptive parents have no guarantees the child will accept them forever, with never a thought of the people who gave him life. This mother sought a child through the process of adoption to love and nurture. She has assumed all the responsibility that role places on her, and she has done so while fully acknowledging "another mother."

Dear Penny,

I have been thinking of you so much, especially since we have celebrated Brandi's 1st birthday. I just know you were thinking of her too.

She started crawling at 9 months and getting into everything. Now she is walking around furniture or if you hold her hands. Her eyes light up with the feeling of accomplishment as she walks. She's very responsive—expressive—you can imagine what she's thinking and chabbering about. Stands on her tip toes a lot, like a little toe dancer. Sometimes balances on one leg while lifting the other. Guess she's going to start climbing soon. Tried to follow her brother up on his bed—fell and looked like she might have her first black eye. It's O.K., just a little redness—don't worry she is a very normal, inquisitive child. She thinks it's real funny to climb up on her brother and pull his hair. She loves to laugh and sometimes fakes laughter for attention. Can cry and squeal real loud too. . . .

I am enclosing a copy of a book that really touched my heart and I pray that it will help you if you ever experience feelings as shared in the book.

I hope you know that you always have the right to be in touch with us or the agency concerning Brandi. And it helps us to know if Brandi ever had

a medical emergency, we could find out about
heritage via the agency. We pray too that you will
stay in touch with the agency so that when Brandi
reaches maturity age and if she wants to contact
you and if agreeable with you, she would be able
to. I pray that you and Brandi never have to suffer
some of the pain and anguish shared in S. Musser's
book.

I have enclosed some pictures of Brandi. As
you can see, she is a joy.

What are your plans for the future? Did you
complete high school or are you starting your senior
year? Hope you are well.

Remember—there is a family you haven't met
who cares for you.

> God bless you,
> Roger and Di
> Bill and Brandi

Birthparents will have no memories of the excitement of
their child's first step, the anxiety of his first day of school,
or the wistful sadness of his graduation from high school.
They relinquish that nurturing parental role. They do not,
however, abandon all responsibility. Birthparents, like the following birthmother, neither forget their children nor do they
want to abdicate whatever role they have in assuring continued security and happiness for their children.

To Clark's Parents,

I'm very glad you were able to write and send
me pictures of Clark. I'm very happy to know that
he is being taken very good care of. From those
ear to ear smiles I can see he is very happy and
happiness is what I always wanted for him.

I'm glad to know he enjoys his big brother so
much. I hope they become very close to each other
as they grow. That would enrich their lives so.

I see the resemblance now between us. He has
my face and his birthfather's muscular body. Clark

sounds like he's going to be an energetic little boy once he starts walking.

It was a happy surprise that you named him Clark. That was the second name I had in mind for him. It is one of my favorite names.

It's a good feeling to know that all is going well and that Clark is growing up the way all little boys should. I hope you keep in touch because it makes me happy to know what a happy and healthy boy he's growing up to be. Please give him a kiss for me and tell him I miss and love him very much. Thank you so much for the letter and the pictures. I really do appreciate it. I'm always hoping only for the best for you and your little family.

Clark's birth mother

When the adoptee finally knows both sets of parents, why should anyone be threatened? If the adoptee grows to love them both, that will not diminish either relationship. Love for one individual is not lessened because we also love another. If knowing and loving gives the adoptee peace of mind, everyone should welcome that opportunity. The child's happiness is the parents' happiness, because the child is the apex of the adoption triangle.

Dear Birthmother,

This has been, at the same time, the most difficult and the easiest letter that we have ever had to write. It is easy to express our love for the baby and our appreciation to you for allowing us to share in that love. It is only the wording which makes it difficult. We keep wondering if phrases like "your baby" or "our baby" will cause anxiety, whereas "the baby" seems so very impersonal. We hope that you will realize that when we refer to "our baby" that you will always be considered as part of that "our," for you will always be a part of her as well as our lives.

It is hard to express how thrilled we were when we received the phone call telling us that our long wait for a baby was finally over. It was, however, nothing compared with the thrill of seeing her for the first time. She is the most beautiful baby girl that we have ever seen. It is possible, I supposed, that we are slightly prejudiced towards her, but that cannot be all of it, as everyone we meet has the same reaction to her. She is not only beautiful, but she is also the sweetest baby that has ever been. She already has such a happy personality, and she is so alert to everything around her. She is amazed by everything she sees and seems completely at ease with every situation.

We know that you must have put a lot of love into the nine months that she was with you, for she could not be any more perfect than she is. She is also very healthy—with not so much as even a simple skin rash. You have enriched our lives far more than any of us can possibly express. Her new brother, who is six, is as excited about her as we are so there will be no end to the amount of love that she will receive.

We hope that you will not feel any sadness upon receiving this letter. You are responsible for so much joy that we hope that some of that joy will be a part of your life as well.

We have enclosed a picture of "our" little girl and her brother. We also wanted to let you know that we had a lovely Baptism service for her on November 9th. We want to wish you the very best that life can bring for you, and express our deepest appreciation for the great joy that you have brought into our lives.

Your friends always,
The Adoptive Parents

9

Openness—
The Opportunity
to Share Love

Dear Birthmother and Friend,

    This is a picture of "our" dear little one. We couldn't let Christmas pass without sharing with you our thoughts and our love. . . .

> Excerpt from a letter
> written by two adoptive
> parents

Since that first letter exchange demanded by a single birthmother, we have taken some big steps forward. Our first step was learning how four myths clouded our thinking and stagnated our adoptive practices. We subsequently abandoned all myths and reevaluated traditional approaches. In the process, our clients taught us to design a program that responds to the needs of all five individuals in the adoption drama. Today, our practices are based on one simple theory:

Individuals handle their lives and their destinies best when addressed with trust and honesty instead of protective secrecy and half truths.

Therefore, we prepare our clients to face the lifetime experience of adoption with faith in themselves and trust for the other members of their triangle.

When we first wrote this book (1980-1982) we avoided the phrase "open adoption" because we were told the term would panic our readers. Since then our clients have convinced us that words do not frighten people; rather, new ideas colliding with preconceived myths frighten people. Individuals who practice traditional adoption or who have experienced a closed adoption do respond to our ideas with skepticism, resentment, or even anger. These reactions are understandable because open adoption directly clashes with the secrecy mandated by the second myth. Although we fully understand and appreciate the cognitive dissonance our approach initially evokes, we no longer hesitate to proudly state that we practice open adoption.

In part, our position is explained by our basic belief that people deal with the truth more quickly and more effectively than with dressed-up words chosen to soften responses, words which also may be chosen to blur realities. We hope this book will serve to enlighten adoption perspectives and assure the reader of the favorable outcomes of open alternatives.

The next question, of course, is how open is "open?" We quickly progressed beyond the simple letter exchanges which we have shared with you in this book to face-to-face meetings, sharing full identifying information (full names and addresses), and ongoing contact over the years. The type and frequency of ongoing contact is determined by the individuals involved in each adoption, but contact ranges from letters and pictures to visitation. In this, our final chapter, we will share these added dimensions of openness.

SHARING NAMES

Today, open adoption includes sharing full names. However, when we began sharing names, we limited this sharing to first names only (unfortunately many agencies call this practice open adoption, while it is, in fact, semi-open adoption). Although it is now difficult for us to remember the depth of our professional concern, we initially worried about and thoroughly discussed the impact of name exchanges.

We assumed birthparents and adoptive parents would both be reticent about exchanging such identifying information. We soon learned that the participants thought differently. Both birthparents and adoptive parents eagerly sought names to erase forever impersonal labels—"your birthparents," "the adoptive parents," "the baby." Somehow, knowing the real names of all the players in their particular adoption story facilitates interaction and intimate sharing among our families. No catastrophes, not even minor injuries, have occurred in the aftermath of what once looked like a great risk. This should serve as a lesson to agencies and other intermediaries who continue to practice semi-open adoption, rather than evolving to fully open adoptions.

Our evolution in exchanging names is an excellent example of how the process and tension of deciding whether to accept an open practice is dramatically overstated when contrasted to its matter-of-fact acceptance today. Now, all parties consider name exchanges as a minimum. In fact, letters that are not addressed to a named person now seem unnatural. The following two letters (and other letters in this chapter), which demonstrate our early name exchanges, chronicle our evolution to increased openness:

Dear Bobbie,

It is very difficult for us to write this letter because we have so many thoughts and so few words to express those thoughts. You gave us the most precious thing in our lives. For this, a simple "thank you" seems so little.

Instead of trying to find some way to tell you how grateful we are for the opportunity to adopt your birthchild, let us instead tell you that he is an extremely happy and contented child. We believe that this happiness begins to develop long before a child is ever born. From you he got this, and that will shape so much of his life. He accepts and gives love so readily with a big smile and sparkling blue eyes.

We appreciate the little stuffed bear and the bear bank that you sent. It is really more than coincidence that you should send bears. You see, we named our son Barret. His room is filled with bears of all sizes and descriptions because his grandfather has already nicknamed him "Bear." In addition to a life-line you have also given him a love-line, and he will be very much aware of this as he grows up.

You are in our prayers, Bobbie, and we hope for you the same happiness that you have given us.

God bless you,
Jenny and John

Dear Jenny and John,

I understand how you feel when you say you cannot express your thoughts and feelings with words. There can be no comparison. You are constantly in my thoughts. I feel very lucky to have such a loving couple as you raise the child I gave birth to. I was so glad to hear he is so happy and loving, and also that he is doing well. I feel his being happy has to do with the environment surrounding him and you have given him that. I would like to thank you for your letter and the picture, I shall treasure them always.

I hope that you won't harbor thoughts of me turning up on your doorstep to take Barret home with me. I have talked to many adopting parents who had this fear. Barret is now your child and no matter what I may feel in the future I will not come searching for him, that choice will be his when he gets older. If he ever decides he feels the need to come and find me, my door will always be open wide for him and you. I feel that as his _real_ parents you are part of me. . . .

I love Barret very much and I know in my heart no one can raise him as well as you can. . . . I have no regrets where Barret is concerned. Of course, I feel, as I'm sure many birthmothers do, that I could have kept him. The Lord had other plans for Barret and myself and we were not meant to be together. I want you to know that when I find that special someone to share my life with, he will know as much as I do about Barret because I want a totally honest relationship. I am not now nor ever will be ashamed of the part I played in giving Barret life. He is a part of me and always will be.

I feel that it's more than coincidence that you named him Barret. I couldn't have given him a better name myself. It seems odd for me to send him bears before I knew his name and what it meant. When I did find out I was pleasantly surprised. I will always think of him as my little (well maybe not so little) "Bear." There is so much more I would like to say but a letter is not the place for it. Words just seem so inadequate for all my feelings and thoughts. I'll just say I love you both and I wish you total happiness in your future. Perhaps with Barret you can find that happiness.

God Bless You,
Bobbie

ONGOING SHARING OF LETTERS AND PHOTOGRAPHS

Our initial letter exchanges contemplated only one exchange in the period immediately following placements. Although we were proud of our "progressive" practice, we never considered that either set of parents might desire continued contact. Adoption triangle members have since taught us differently. Today, the number of periodic letter exchanges depends on the individuals involved in each case. Most of our clients now communicate on a regular basis, the child's birthday and Christmas being special days. Letters exchanged usually focus on developmental information about the adoptee and expressions of concern and assurance between the two sets of parents. The following letter is a good example of both. The letter was written by a young adoptive couple to their son's birthmother one and one-half years after Alan's placement. They sought to update Irene about Alan, since their first letter had been written when Alan was only four months old:

Dear Irene,

Please forgive this late overdue letter. We think of you daily and pray for your happiness. But we live out of state now by our families and Alan is so attached to his grandparents and cousins. He is the only grandson on his dad's side of the family. He can do no wrong with them.

Alan is such a happy little boy. He loves to flirt with girls in the stores. They comment on his dimple and he winks at them. His favorite toys are tonka trucks and books on trucks.

His health has been excellent this year. Last year he had a few ear infections. He is a very active little guy. We joke about him either taking something apart; trying to plug it in; or putting it back together. He's very coordinated for his size. We think he will be a good athlete if that's what he wants. He has a very good memory for things he has seen and then tries it at a later time. He really keeps us on the go, and we love it.

Alan has made our family so complete. His sisters love him, and he goes to them for protection if he is in the wrong. Alan is a wonderful little boy that you can be very proud of. He also has a very kind side that loves little babies and shares very well.

He goes once a week to a play group. If another child cries, Alan will pat that child's back or kiss them. His teacher is very impressed by his thoughtfulness at this early age.

A simple "thank you" just isn't enough for this wonderful little boy. You can be sure we'll try to raise him to be a happy well adjusted child and to have a healthy understanding of his adoption. We feel very strong that Alan will love you just as we do as he matures. May God be with you and your family. Have a happy holiday.

Happy Holidays,
Betty and Stan

Birthparents who receive updates about their child cherish the information and the warmth of the letters. For some who feel isolated from society for being unwed parents, these letters become their only outlet for their continued caring. Dawn responded to a letter from her child's adoptive parents by assuring them she did not intend to infringe on their family's happiness, but was thankful to them for "showing me that the biggest decision of my life that I had to make was the right one. . . ."

Dearest Nancy and Terry,

I can't begin to tell you how much fulfillment and happiness your letter and darling pictures brought to me.

Your letter relieved a lot of thoughts and most important my decision to relinquish "our son." I agree very strongly that Drew is our baby. I brought Drew into this world and you gave him a home of love, happiness and health. I couldn't ask for anything more.

Drew is a beautiful baby. I thank you so very much for the pictures. I can see by the smile on his face he is indeed a happy, content and healthy little boy. I will treasure Drew's pictures and your very kind and thoughtful letter for a very long time.

Your letter was just that very kind and thoughtful. I especially appreciate you sharing with me, how Drew is progressing with his first two years of life.

There also is rarely a day that goes by, I don't think of Drew, now I can add his parents to my thoughts with thanks of knowing that Drew will receive nothing but the best throughout his life.

I want you to understand that you will receive no trouble from me and I would deeply appreciate it if you would stay in touch every so often, and would share a few of Drew's pictures with me. I know that is a lot to ask and I'll understand if you don't agree. It's just a wonderful feeling seeing what an adorable child Drew is and know that the three of you are doing fine. For the three of you are a big and important part of my life. My hopes and prayers will always be with you.

At one time I was considering writing Drew a letter to be put away until his 18th birthday, explaining the reason why I gave him up for adoption. I have now changed my mind. I have only one favor to ask of you, and that is to explain to Drew, for me, when the time is right, or best, the reason I made the decision, and that was, because at seventeen I couldn't of provided him with a proper home, nor a father figure, he left long ago. The love for Drew was so strong at that time, that Drew came first. That's when I made my decision to let go of Drew and give him to a couple who could give him all the love and comforts of a home and the joys of life. I will never expect Drew to think of me as a mother, for you are the only parents he'll grow to know and love. I do want Drew to understand I did and do love him, and because of that I wanted to give him the best which I am convinced I did.

My life has gone on. I just finished a year of college and plan on transferring over to a business college. I also plan to marry in a years' time and am looking forward to starting a family of my own in the future.

My mother wants to send her thanks for the pictures and the letter. She thought Drew's pictures were darling, and the letter was very considerate.

Yes, I have faith in God, for he gave us Drew. I, too, agree we'll all be Drew's parents in heaven.

May God Bless and Watch over you and Drew.

Thank you, Thank you for showing me that the biggest decision of my life that I had to make was the right one and it gave happiness to three other people, Drew, Nancy and Terry. God Bless and Be with you. All my love and gratitude.

Dawn

P.S. Drew is a beautiful name. I really like it.

In turn, adoptive parents like Nancy and Terry enthusiastically seek ongoing correspondence with their son's birthmother. The reasons include a desire to repay the birthmother for her gift of a child and the hope that such open communication will benefit their child's growth and identity.

Ongoing correspondence also provides the adoptee access to a complete genealogical history and current medical records of both the birthmother and the birthfather. The following letter is one in the series of exchanges Nancy and Terry have shared with Dawn. Their letter (in answer to another one of Dawn's letters) is typical of the concern and love we see shared:

Dear Dawn,

We were so excited, so curious, so delighted and so touched to get your letter!! You are so pretty and Drew looks so much like you!

We are going to keep one picture out for Drew to see often and take one picture to a safe deposit box, along with your letters, for safe keeping.

It was so wonderful to hear all about your life now. It sounds as though things are really shaping up for you. Terry and I are really happy about your upcoming graduation and marriage. I know the new year is going to be your year!

Everything is very exciting here. Drew, Terry and I are anxiously awaiting a new baby that we are all adopting. Of course we don't know when the baby will come but we hope it's in time for Christmas! We tell Drew about adopting another baby but we're not sure he understands. But when we babysit our two month old niece, Kelly, Drew really enjoys her and is not jealous at all. Of course Drew has always been King around here! He was the first grandchild on my side and when relatives visit, "BOY," does he get the attention!

Drew is short for Robert Andrew which is his whole name. Everyone warned us that two years of age would be terrible. But on the contrary, this is Drew's cutest age ever! He can talk to us in a combination of words and gestures. He is <u>extremely</u> loving and kisses and hugs us constantly. Daddy is his favorite person and he imitates him perfectly. When Terry goes on trips—(he's an airplane pilot) Drew says "Daddy flying" and makes a gesture and a sound like an airplane. He does this about ten times a day! He loves flying in airplanes and of course we travel a lot. Drew has been in many states. He's crazy about giraffes and goes wild over them at the zoo!

Terry and I are wondering whether we could love another child as much as we love Drew but both of our mothers assure us that we can (Terry's mom has 6 sons and my mom has 5 children).

We think of you daily, Dawn, and we pray for your well being. Especially when my sister-in-law was pregnant and I saw her physical and emotional stages and I realized what you went through for Drew and for us. Never having been pregnant, I had never before realized the degree of sacrifice and love you must have experienced and felt. I guess we can never repay you fully. The one thing we can and will do is to raise "our" son to the very best of our abilities and give our all to this goal!

The more you write to us about you the more we grow in our love for you. Drew will be the most benefited from your letters, though. I can't wait until he's old enough to comprehend the love you have for him.

You have a very unique place in our lives. You gave Terry and me the gift of a life and for that we will always love you! Of course, we all know who ultimately gave us Drew, but you were His earthly counterpart.

It just proves that Romans 8:28 "God works all things together for good. . . ." is true. I'm sure when you first found out you were pregnant, not much seemed good about it, but just look at the happiness you've brought us!

As for Drew's great pair of legs that you referred to in your letter—What an understatement—He has the cutest, strongest, chubbiest legs ever.

Terry wanted to add to this but got called out on a trip and we wanted to get this to you quickly! But he'll write next time!

Have a wonderful Christmas! We love you.

Terry, Nancy and Drew

Our initial open practices carefully excluded identifying information. Pictures of the baby were encouraged because birthparents so obviously benefited. Babies change, however, so we somehow felt safe. What we did not realize at first was how the myths still motivated us. We unconsciously sought safe exchanges even though we no longer believed secrecy was best. Actually, our adoptive parents spontaneously changed this by first sending current pictures of the adoptee to birthparents, and then by venturing to request current pictures of the birthparents. Today, our clients share fully. Birthparents can choose to receive a variety of pictures of their baby and pictures of his adoptive parents. Adoptive parents, in return, can obtain pictures of their child's birthparents and extended family members.

Once again, the afterglow of these picture exchanges has been positive. Triangle members express delight in being able to visualize each other as real people. Adoptive parents remain the most enthusiastic, safeguarding the pictures for their children. Many adoptive parents, in fact, place the birthparents' names and pictures in the adoptee's baby book. These thus become an integral and natural part of that child's story. Some adoptive parents put the birthmother's picture in the baby's room—on his dresser or hanging on the wall (just as other relatives' pictures are displayed throughout the house).

As we evolved with open adoption, so did most of our previous clients. When Beverly and Kent adopted their daughter, Kelly, they were only interested in an initial letter. Since then, as their letter demonstrates, they have done volunteer work with birthparents and read extensively on current adoption controversies. Their awareness of the benefits of open approaches is reflected in the following letter to their birthparents, which is their third such letter:

Dear Birthparents,

I am sure this letter and these pictures out of the unexpected will surprise you. I sincerely hope they will be a happy surprise.

In the past year we have become more involved in the adoption agency serving as a volunteer foster family for several young women as they waited for the birth of their babies. I'm sure this association has brought about a deeper understanding of birthmothers. I have also watched the changing procedures within the agency in regard to more openness between birthparents and adoptive families, openness which has included exchange of pictures, names and even face-to-face meetings.

These experiences have resulted in wanting to share these pictures and in writing again to keep open communication. I am sure you must wonder about this beautiful daughter and how she is developing. I chose these pictures which were taken in April on an outing in the wildflowers at Canyon Lake because they are favorites of both her mother and father. One picture seems to capture the joyous spirit that she is and the other lets you see how beautiful she really is. I hope there is joy for you in these pictures. We would find joy in receiving pictures of you.

We also have learned that you named your daughter Amy. This was shared by the foster family. I am thrilled to know this name and our daughter will know also that her "first" name is Amy. Did you give her a middle name? We have named her Kelly Anne.

Our social worker also shared with us the news that you married. We were happy for you and wish you happiness and joy in your life together. We are appreciative of any information about you that we have in anticipation of all the questions that Kelly will someday have and plan to be completely open with her in all that we know. I am also open to giving you continued updates on her development.

We are now in the process of applying for another baby so Kelly will not be an only child. We have been asked if we would be open to a face-to-face meeting with the birthmother. While the idea was initially unsettling, knowing how much I would love a face-to-face meeting with you I am hoping that opportunity will become a reality with the next child we adopt.

Our daughter is developing beautifully. She is into climbing these days. When I leave the room for a minute, it is not unusual to return and find her sitting in the middle of the table playing with whatever she found there "safely" out of her reach. She is saying lots of words such as wow, eye, bye bye, shoes, juice, grandma and so on. Unfortunately at this point her favorite seems to be "no" whether she means it or not.

Again, I want to express to you our gratitude for the chance to parent and love this most wonderful daughter of ours. So often we watch her and tell each other how rich we are. She is all we hoped for and more. We thank you and wish you joy and peace in your lives.

Sincerely yours,
Beverly and Kent

MEETING FACE-TO-FACE

When *Dear Birthmother* was initially published, only a few adoption agencies in the country allowed face-to-face meetings between adoptive parents and the birthparents of their baby at or near the time of placement. Today, many adoptions include at least a one-time face-to-face meeting, and progressive adoption programs offer open adoption (which includes meeting, sharing full identifying information, and having access to ongoing contact over the years). After many years of facilitating face-to-face meetings, we feel strongly that these meetings and direct ongoing contact benefit all adoption triangle members.

At the initial meeting, which is typically while the birthmother is still pregnant, all participants come together with respect for each other's role, and with some trepidation. Birthparents leave the meeting having learned more about the people who will provide the nurturing aspects of parenthood to their baby. As a result, birthparents do not have to labor under a lifetime guilt for having "abandoned" their child. They instead remember having actually participated in making responsible plans for that child's future.

One birthmother wrote the following love-inspired poem to the adoptive parents of her son after their face-to-face meeting.

> *I know we've only just met*
> *But feelings of love do exist,*
> *For circumstances of*
> *   future and past*
> *Have given opportunities*
> *   that our lives may share—*
> *And though our paths may vary,*
> *   We have a common goal*
> *For a child to grow happy*
> *   and healthy and wise—*
> *In a home that I have chosen.*
>
> D. L. Click
> Birthmother

Adoptive parents also leave the meetings having learned more about the birthparents. Fears of mysterious strangers are dissipated, and remaining stereotypes of "those kinds of people" are effectively destroyed. Adoptive parents also learn valuable firsthand facts about the birthparent's interests and true personality, the kind of characteristics that can not be captured in a written social history. We often feel and hear their excitement in the simple statement, "I can tell my daughter I really met her birthmother."

The following note was written by an adoptive father, explaining his feelings about his initial meeting with Kim, his sons's birthmother, shortly after the adoption:

I was pleasantly surprised to find the birthmother of my adopted son, Daniel, to be prettier and more intelligent than I thought she would be. I don't know why I would have pre-conceived notions that she wouldn't be, unless I was preparing myself, in case she turned out to be that way.

From my standpoint, it was a beautiful event of sharing information, getting to know and understand each other a little, and an opportunity I will never forget.

I now have the opportunity of telling Daniel what his mother is really like. Of course she will grow and mature, but it may help him understand a little better why she had to give him up and that she could not have provided the kind of life for him that she really wants him to have, at least not at this time of her life.

There didn't seem to be any barriers between us and it did help to find a subject that we all had in common besides the baby. That was cats! Once we hit that subject, we got into all sorts of topics, mostly about Kim.

The experience of getting to know Kim will benefit our family for years to come and probably in some ways we haven't thought of yet. It seems to make the adoption process more complete and satisfying and I feel that Kim benefited greatly from the meeting too.

The only thing that I found was different from what I expected was the fact that we didn't sit around and stare at each other for awhile before we could think of anything to say. It was easy to bring up subjects, ask questions, and give answers freely. . . .

I want to thank the agency for giving us the opportunity to have this meeting. If they were not

progressive in their ideas, we would not have had
this opportunity and we would never have gotten
to know a beautiful young woman named Kim.
                                    Greg

Other adoptive parents who have met with their birthparents have spoken in the same positive terms as Daniel's
adoptive father. To date they have expressed only one disad-
vantage. Without exception they have all encountered from
family members and friends troubled reactions to these meetings. They have often heard such comments as "Aren't you
afraid that, now that she knows who you are, she will come
get your baby back?" or "I could never do that!" By contrast,
the parents who have had the most direct experience, felt
reassured and comfortable with their meetings. They have
had the unique opportunity to see and hear their birthparents
personally say, "I won't interfere," or "I no longer feel that
she is just my baby," or "I love you both."

One adoptive father emotionally touched by the
experience of meeting his son's birthmother wrote a letter to
his son to be read and appreciated at some future date. He
and his wife first met the birthmother, Lori, during her pregnancy, visited with her and the baby in the hospital, and continued to visit after the adoption (Lori came to spend her
Easter vacation with them). They plan to continue with regular visits and correspondence over the years. The letter cap-
tures the adoptive father's affection and trust for the woman
who is Neil's birthmother:

Dearest Neil,
        As your mother and I look at your smiling,
happy face, our thoughts rush out to another happy,
smiling face in our lives. Your birthmother, Lori,
is a wonderful, beautiful person who has become
an important part of all of our lives.
        We will always remember the day we first met
Lori. She was far more nervous than your mother
or I. She after all, had read our autobiographies,
and was certain that she would like us. She was

afraid, however, that we would reject her and not feel comfortable raising her child.

We did not know very much about her beyond the brief background information given to us by our social worker. We did see a picture of your birthparents, and were impressed with how handsome they looked together.

Lori did not stay nervous very long. She is such a warm, outgoing person that she rapidly put everyone at ease. It was so easy to like Lori, after all, she has your dimples and smile.

Lori was very concerned about your future and for that reason she selected your mother and I to raise you. Lori wanted you to be loved and to be raised by parents who shared her interests in athletics and education. She wanted you nurtured by a family that would love you as much as she does.

We want you to appreciate how exciting it was for your mother and I to again visit you and Lori the day after your birth. That time in the hospital is special and is shared by very few adoptive families. Lori was so proud of you when she took us to the nursery to see you. We remember how small you were and what a tight bundle the nurses had made of you and your blankets. Your mother was worried that we would not find you as beautiful as Lori did. We worried that Lori's pride in you was caused by her love for you, but as soon as we saw you we knew that Lori had every right to be proud. You were a very beautiful, healthy baby. Lori told us how much you looked like pictures she had seen of her sister and herself as babies.

The next day was very special for our new family. Lori brought you from the hospital to the agency where your mother and I waited. We had a ceremony during which Lori presented you to us and asked us to love you and care for you.

You know that your mother and I correspond with Lori very often. She has become part of all our lives and will always play a role in your life.

The pictures and letters we exchange with one another are treasured by all of us. She has become a good friend who shares our love for you.

Your mother and I are very comfortable with our lives as adoptive parents. We are proud of you and relate the story of your adoption to anyone who asks. Some people, who hear our story for the first time, are troubled because in the past birthparents and adoptive families were not allowed to correspond or meet face to face. When they understand our story, and learn how important it is for you to know about the couple who gave you birth, they realize that adoption affects more than just three people. It affects the adoptive parent's family and the birthparent's families. Communicating with your birthparents keeps their families aware of your development. Hopefully this will draw all of our families closer together. Our closeness will make it easier for you to receive answers to the questions you will have as you grow older.

We want you to always know that many people love you. Among those who love you most are your mother and I and a very special young woman who loved you very much when you were born and who loves you still. We know when you are older you will return the love that all of us have invested in you.

All our love,
Your parents

When we began to offer face-to-face meetings, many of our past adoptive parents and birthparents who did not get this opportunity expressed an interest in meeting one another. One such couple, Terry and Nancy, whom we met earlier in this chapter, invited their first birthmother to meet with them after they had the experience of meeting with the birthmother of their second child, Sarah. The letter that Dawn, the birthmother, wrote in response to Terry and Nancy's unexpected request dramatically speaks of the

bond of love these individuals so freely and comfortably want
to share:

> Hi Terry, Nancy and Drew,
>
> Let me congratulate you on the new addition,
> Sarah Beth, what a beautiful name for such a beau-
> tiful little girl. She is adorable. I'm so happy to hear
> that Drew adores her and there is no sign of jealousy.
> I know that makes it a lot easier on the whole family.
>
> No, I couldn't believe that you got to meet
> Sarah's birthmother. Wow, that's great, I mean that
> is wonderful. I'm still a little shocked. How I wish
> that I would of had that priviledge. I'm not really
> jealous of the fact that Gail met with you and saw
> Sarah, but I am serious, I actually cried when I
> read in your letter that I could meet you and see
> Drew. Oh, Terry and Nancy I need no time to think
> whether or not I would like to meet with you and
> Drew (and of course I would love to meet Sarah,
> after all she is Drew's sister).
>
> That has been my biggest prayer and dream
> and one of my most thought of thoughts. I would
> love to meet with you. The only problem is it can't
> be right now. It would have to be either this sum-
> mer say August or this winter around November.
> If that could be arranged. The reason is one school,
> I don't graduate till June. Then hopefully I will
> get a job. Job means money and money means my
> plane ticket to San Antonio. Would that be okay with
> you. You know that I will try to meet with you
> as soon as possible. I think this is wonderful. You
> don't know how happy it would make me feel. I feel
> that since we all feel that we know each (in my
> opinion) other quite well, we would have little, maybe
> even no trouble picking up the pieces. I'm sure we'd
> feel comfortable. In your letter (it was a lovely let-
> ter I read it 2 times then I read it to my mom!)
> you said meet now, please let me know if August
> or November—somewhere in between there would
> be too late to make our arrangements. It's the best

I can do, I hope and pray that it will all work out. It's all we've been thinking about. If you'd like you can also tape our conversation. Ask anything you'd like, especially anything concerning Drew and his future because you are the only ones I would talk to about Drew's natural father. Listen to me I'm so excited, I better stop getting so carried away and wait to hear what you have to say about our arrangement. I just know there is nothing I want more than to meet Drew and talk to him, hold and kiss him and meet the two most very special people that God has given to me.

I also feel deep down in my heart that there is a bond between Gail and I. I feel that she is very special. We've both been through the same situation, experienced the same experiences, and were both blessed with beautiful healthy babies that God put into the care of two wonderful people named Nancy and Terry. I too feel that God put us together ultimately and I love Him that much more for His miracles.

I love the two pictures that you sent me. Drew has grown, I should say is growing. He looks like he's a little taller than most boys his age. He is so cute. My mother said she thought the picture of Terry, Drew and Sarah was adorable. She especially liked your caption on the back. Nancy, if I haven't mentioned it before my mother is also very comfortable with our situation. We often sit down and talk for hours about my pregnancy and how happy Drew looks in his pictures. Our favorite conversation is talking about how cute Drew is.

She has been a big help to me especially when I returned home from San Antonio. We would talk, she was mainly concerned with how I was going to deal with the act after relinquishing our son. She says she is very proud of me for my decision and how I've handled myself. She too was hurting at first after all Drew at that time may of been her grandson. Now she feels that God worked it all out for the best. I'm the kind of person who likes to talk things out. I don't hold things in. My being like this has opened many doors for me. Giving birth to Drew made me realize many things most of all I have learned and matured from that. I know that I am going to do my darndest to fulfill my life and those involved and around me. Life is too precious to waste. I have high hopes for me starting a family. May I (when the time comes to start a family) share this with you. You will always be with me for the rest of my life (you won't be able to get rid of me, I love you all too much).

Drew's nursery school seems like it is really neat—as you put it.

I was excited to hear that Drew's teacher said that he is well adjusted and secure. It's very important to me how Drew will adjust as he grows. I have total confidence in you. But it does make me feel great to hear comments about him, especially one as important as that was.

I know we said it over and over but I have to say it one more time. I am so glad God blessed Drew with a wonderful mother and father. I wouldn't want him with anyone else.

I hope this letter was understandable. My mind is still a little in shock about the new concept at the agency—Boy that's great. I do hope and pray we will meet, not right now, but real soon. (Hope!) I've got my fingers crossed.

Again, thank you for the picture of Drew and Sarah and Terry. They will be added to the rest. I will try to send pictures too.

> I love you lots,
> Dawn

SHARING FULL IDENTIFYING INFORMATION AND ONGOING VISITATION

Open adoption includes not only meeting one another, but also sharing full identifying information and ongoing contact over the years. The bond which develops between adoptive parents and birthparents continues beyond the time of the adoption, because these individuals care about one another (in fact, they even love one another). Therefore, they want to maintain a relationship with one another. In effect, as mentioned in *Children of Open Adoption*, they relate to one another like relatives. Yes, the birthmother is a relative because she is related to the child. Recognition of this fact is what open adoption is all about—accepting the birthparents (and their family) into your life as extended family members.

A few months after Larry and Darlene wrote their "Birthmother Letter" (Chapter 7), they were selected by a birthmother, Lisa, who was in the ninth month of her pregnancy at the time. They met and felt an instant bonding with one another. Darlene recalls some of their initial fears about open adoption and discusses the evolution of their special relationship:

> We signed up for an orientation meeting ... We walked out after four hours of listening intently, got in our car and said, "This isn't for us! No matter how bad we wanted a baby and to know the birthparents, this is crazy." The more we talked about it, we said let's give it a shot. We know so many people and family out of state that we would send our birthmother letter out of state, so we could match up with a birthmother from the east coast, fly her here to have the baby, and then fly her home. We thought this would be ideal for us. ... We attended the two workshop sessions at the Center. We listened to the birthparents and adoptive parents (with open adoptions). My heart went out to them. You could feel all their emotions as though you had been through them yourself. ...

The experience of the educational process and meeting their birthmother Lisa ("We all seemed so relaxed— as though we had known each other for years") changed their views dramatically. All of a sudden they were delighted to have a local birthmother (rather than one who would be 3,000 miles away). They even invited Lisa to their first family baby shower shortly after Joey's birth, which also helped their families get to know and trust Lisa. Darlene recalls that as her family members were leaving the shower, "They all gave Lisa a hug and said 'Thank you.' But my greatest gift was watching my Mom and Larry's Mom both hug, kiss, and share tears with Lisa."

During the first few months post-birth, Darlene and Larry continued to visit with Lisa on a regular basis. In fact, they got upset when they didn't hear from Lisa as often as they wanted, so they bought her a telephone answering machine so they could leave messages telling her to call them!

Darlene and Larry have accepted Lisa into their lives as an extended family member, and they have a special love for her. Lisa worked through the normal feelings of grief much more easily because of her ongoing relationship with Joey and his parents. Joey reaps the benefit of having a relationship with both sets of parents. Today, two years after Joey's birth, their relationship (and love for one another) continues to grow, and they look forward to continuing to visit over the years.

Two years after Joey's birth, Lisa shares her feelings about their initial meeting and their ongoing relationship:

> I will never forget ther first time I saw Larry and Darlene together. It was the day of our match meeting (initial meeting facilitated by the adoption counselor), and we had pulled in about the same time. I saw both of them, and I wanted to cry—not out of sadness, but because I wanted everything to be okay for them. I felt I loved them, and it was an instant bonding, and it was wonderful. Joey kept kicking inside me (inside my stomach) as if he was saying "Yes! Yes! Go for it!"
>
> I had prayed before to help me pick the right people. God really listened. I picked the best in my opinion. I thank God for them everyday. They gave me a new beginning, as I did for them. It was the

most beautiful natural solution to my confusion, and my life was starting to fall together. I felt good about myself finally.

The next morning Joey was born. I was unsure if I even wanted to hold him. They brought this beautiful baby boy to my room. Larry held him first, I wanted it that way, since I truly believe in bonding. Besides Darlene was shaking like a leaf and hugging my mom. I was so happy for all of us.

They left about an hour later, and I decided to hold Joey. I held him, talked to him, and explained why. He looked as if he was saying, "I'm happy, it's okay, I understand."

If it had been a closed adoption, my heart would have been torn to pieces. I'd always be worried and wondering about him. With open adoption, I know he is so loved. My relationship with Larry and Darlene is incredible. I've gained a wonderful addition to my loved ones. We are like family. I call them about everything. They always support me and give me good advice, too. I can count on them. It's not as if I call them daily, drilling them on Joey's life. I call because I am loved and worried about. We get together about once a month.

We have a very loving, healthy relationship, and I feel very blessed. I love them all very much. If I hadn't become pregnant, I would have never met these 2 wonderful people who have enriched my life. I think trust is the key here.

P. S. Darlene and Larry you're the BEST!!

Sandy, an adoptive mother, shared an early letter to their birthmother, Colleen, in Chapter 2. Now several years later, they continue to write to one another, talk on the phone ("It's been great to just pick up the phone and hear her voice or be able to call on special days"), and visit periodically. Sandy relates her feelings about their relationship and about Jed's (age 8 1/2) special birthday request:

In October Jed asked if we could go someplace special for his birthday month (November). When we asked him what he had in mind, he said he wanted to visit Colleen. . . .

Colleen suggested Sea World in San Antonio so neither of us would have to travel a long distance. It was a wonderful day for all of us with many talks, especially about what Colleen wanted for her future. . . .

She loved to compare Jed's special interests to those she had as a child and still has. There are many they have in common. . .

We have a closeness that includes trust and concern for each other. We have all felt very comfortable with each other and have felt mutual respect.

Jed feels loved by Colleen and does not seem confused about her relationship to him. Our openness with Jed and Colleen has made our family relationship richer and has dispelled any fear or apprehension that we felt just before our first meeting.

Another adoptive mother, Caryl shares their evolution from semi-open adoption to open adoption:

Seven and a half years ago, my husband and I would never have believed that we would ever invite our son's birthmother to our home for dinner along with her brother and his family, including her in our traditional celebration of the day we got him, nor think of her as part of our extended family. However, all of these things have occurred and more.

When we first agreed to an open adoption, we were willing to have one face-to-face meeting and to share letters anonymously through the adoption agency. Our first meeting occurred four days after the placement, and despite our anxiety and fear of the unknown, we immediately felt comfortable with John's birthmother. We found we had many similarities in our feelings regarding our own families, enjoyed the same activities, and placed the same value on many aspects of our lives. Corresponding with Colette, John's birth-mother, served to deepen this relationship because we gradually began to realize that we were not adversaries but partners who wanted the same things for John: happy, loving relationships in which he would grow and find his own uniqueness.

This relationship developed as we grew to know and trust each other. . . . We realized his understanding of this (Colette's relationship to him) when he asked if we could invite her to our annual celebration of the day we got him. The importance of this risk for all of us is the way John has accepted the honesty and love that he has received. He enjoys knowing his birth-mother and is a secure, happy child. As we look to the future, we have many questions and concerns about the effects on John and his acceptance of Colette; however, we do not have the fear we had seven and a half years ago. We feel confidence in our relationship and our ability to adjust to John's changing needs.

BEYOND THE MYTHS

Because our evolution has been dramatic when contrasted to traditional adoptive practices, we have carefully evaluated each of our steps. Interestingly, whether it be letters, names, pictures, or meetings, the only difficulty for the triangle members has been dealing with the comments of individuals outside the triangle—misguided friends, well-meaning family, and even some less progressive professionals. Our clients typically understand these comments and can patiently handle the reactions because they vividly remember when they too responded to adoption with the prejudices of the four adoption myths. Indeed, our triangle members become ambassadors and teachers to lead others to reject outmoded and often damaging ideas.

Epilogue

Our advocacy of open adoption practices often evokes two questions—whether from adoptive parents, physicians, judges, newspaper reporters, or casual onlookers:

- Who really benefits from the openness?
- Won't open adoption have a chilling effect on the practice of adoption?

We answer the first question easily. The adoptee is our primary concern and stands to benefit most. As a child, he needs roots to grow, these being a permanent home and the security of a loving family. As an adult, he may need to know his genetic roots. Therefore, our task is to prepare both sets of parents. We want his birthparents to live with pride for the active participation they took in making responsible plans for their birthchild. We also want his adoptive parents to take pride in their status as parents. That includes having enough confidence in themselves and the adoptee's love to show him that they won't be crushed or think him ungrateful if he searches for the missing pieces of his own precious identity.

We address the second question by sharing the experiences and growth of the men and women living today's adoption stories. Our clients dramatically communicate to us that they are enriched and excited by our practices. It is possible for questioners or opponents to label our birthparents and adoptive parents as unique and special, saying, "These are not average individuals. They don't react the same way most people would in a similar situation." Not so. These are ordinary men and women, exceptional only in that they have had the opportunity to experience and react to adoption in a myth-free manner.

What we offer our readers—and society—is a workable approach to make future adoptions more humane and appropriately open in today's world. As we have witnessed open adoptions over the years since *Dear Birthmother* was initially published, we have become even more convinced that open adoption is healthier for all parties. We encourage our readers to seek out a professional intermediary who offers both open adoption and comprehensive counseling services. We feel that counseling, education, and support services are essential to a successful open adoption and should be an *intregal* part of any adoption program.

We wrote this book partly to applaud adoptive relationships that are open and trusting. Adults seem to have more trouble with trusting. Children, on the other hand, appear naturally free in their acceptance and expressions. We feel the following three letters appropriately end our book. The first two letters were written by a nine-year-old and a seven-year-old to the birthmother of their new brother. In the simple and unabashed outpouring of real feelings, these two youngsters see adoption only as a wonderful opportunity to share love.

Dear BirthMother

thank you for letting us
adottopt   your baby

he is very   cute.
We LOVE him very
very very very very
very much. I like toomake
him laugh and make
him say words. He
is very healthy.
I like to see
him eat his
food cause
he is cute
then. trn it
over

I like to put him in to his
baby swing and get him out
of his bed and hold him to. I
like to stroll him around.

and also he sleeps most of the
day time and he is very pleasant
when he sleeps

from your baby's
brother age 7

Dear Birthmother,

Your baby is right beside me watching me write this note to you.

He is the healthiest, happiest, smartest and most wanted baby (I think) in the whole world.

We have enjoyed him so so so much these two months. Already I feel like he's been here at our house for a long time.

I love his laugh and I love him, he's the sweetest baby.

Lovingly,
His adoptive sister

age 9 going on 10

Our last letter, from Cara Speedlin, age 11, who engages in ongoing visitation and other communication with her birthmother, demonstrates how children who are living with open adoption consider this to be "normal" adoption (as discussed further in *Children of Open Adoption*):

Dear Birthmother (Liz),

I think open adoption is very satisfying. I think this way of adoption is better than closed adoption because you know who gave birth to you and you at least know who your father is.

Birthmother, I'm glad you chose open adoption. I remember the first time we met. Do you? I remember how much fun we had. You and Kenny were the greatest. I'm thankful that you named my half-sister after me.

All these things could not have been possible without open adoption. I hope to continue to communicate with you.

Love,
Cara Elizabeth Speedlin
(age 11)

Recommended Reading

Arms, Suzanne, *Adoption: A Handful of Hope*, Berkeley, Celestial Arts, 1989 (originally published as *To Love and Let Go*)

Gritter, Jim, editor, *Adoption Without Fear*, San Antonio, Corona Publishing Co., 1989

Halverson, Kaye with Karen M. Hess, *The Wedded Unmother*, Minneapolis, Augsburg Publishing House, 1980

Johnston, Patricia Irwin, *An Adoptor's Advocate*, Ft. Wayne IN, Perspectives Press, 1984

Kirk, H. David, *Adoptive Kinship*, Toronto, Butterworth & Co., 1981

————, *Shared Fate: A Theory of Adoption and Mental Health*, New York, The Free Press, 1964

Lifton, Betty Jean, *Lost and Found*, New York, Harper & Row, 1988

Lindsay, Jeanne Warren, *Open Adoption: A Caring Option*, Buena Park CA, Morning Glory Press, 1987

Lindsay, Jeanne Warren and Catherine Monserrat, *Adoption Awareness*, Buena Park CA, Morning Glory Press, 1989

Melina, Lois Ruskai, *Raising Adopted Children*, New York, Harper & Row, 1986

Menning, Barbara Eck, *Infertility: A Guide for the Childless Couple*, Englewood Cliffs NJ, Prentice-Hall, Inc., 1977

Musser, Sandra Kay, *I Would Have Searched Forever*, Plainfield NJ, Haven Books, 1979

Pannor, Reuben and Annette Baran, "Open Adoption As Standard Practice," *Child Welfare*, New York, Child Welfare League of America, Inc., Volume LXIII, Number 3, May-June 1984

Rappaport, Bruce M., "The Normalization of Adoption," *New Adoption Journal*, Pleasant Hill CA, Independent Adoption Center, Summer/Fall Edition 1988

Rillera, Mary Jo and Sharon Kaplan, *Cooperative Adoption*, Westminster CA, Triadoption Publications, 1984

Silber, Kathleen and Patricia Martinez Dorner, *Children of Open Adoption*, San Antonio, Corona Publishing Co., 1990

Sorosky, Arthur D., Annette Baran, and Reuben Pannor, *The Adoption Triangle*, San Antonio, Corona Publishing Co., 1989

Stephenson, Mary, *My Child Is a Mother*, San Antonio, Corona Publishing Co., 1991

Verny, Thomas, M.D., with John Kelly, *The Secret Life of the Unborn Child*, New York, A Delta Book, 1981

Wishard, Laurie and William Wishard, *Adoption: The Grafted Tree*, San Francisco, Cragment, 1979

Books for Children

Girard, Linda Walvoord, *Adoption Is For Always*, Niles IL, Albert Whitman & Co., 1986

Krementz, Jill, *How It Feels to be Adopted*, New York, Knopf, 1982

Lifton, Betty Jean, *I'm Still Me*, New York, Bantam Books, Inc., 1981

Livingston, Carole, *Why Was I Adopted?* Secaucus NJ, Lyle Stuart, Inc., 1978

Nerlove, Evelyn, *Who Is David?* New York, Child Welfare League of America, 1985

Sly, Kathleen O'Connor, *Becky's Special Family*, Corona CA, Alternative Parenting Publications, 1985

The Dream Fast
Anishinabe

Long ago, as it still is today, it was the custom for a boy who reached a certain age to go into the forest and wait for a dream. He would build a small lodge and go without food for many days, in the hope he would be visited by some animal or spirit of the forest that would take pity on him and give guidance and power.

There was a boy named Opichi who reached that age. Opichi's father was very respected in the village, and he was determined that his son would be given a dream of such power that no one else could compare with him. So eager was the father for his son to get power that he insisted the boy go on his dream fast before the last snow left the ground, even though most boys would wait until the time when the ground was warm and the leaves returned to the trees.

"My son is strong," said the father. "He will go now. He will gain greater strength from the cold."

Opichi was a boy who always wished to please his parents, and so he did as his father said. They went together into the forest, and the father selected a spot on top of a small hill. There Opichi made a small lean-to of saplings, covering it with hemlock boughs. He sat beneath it on the bare ground with a thin piece of deerskin wrapped about his shoulders.

"I will return each day at dawn," the father said. "You will tell me then what you have seen."

That night the north wind, the icy breath of the Great Bear, blew cold. Opichi's mother was concerned, but the father did not worry. "My son is strong," he said. "This cold wind will make his vision a better one."

When the morning came, he went to the lean-to and shook the poles.

"My son," he said, "tell me what you have seen."

Opichi crawled out and looked up at his father. "Father," the boy said, "a deer came to the lodge and spoke to me."

"That is good," said his father. "But you must continue to fast. Surely a greater vision will come to you."

"I will continue to watch and wait," Opichi said.

Opichi's father left his son and went back to his lodge. That night a light snow fell. "I am worried about our son," said Opichi's mother.

"Do not worry," said the father. "The snow will only make whatever dream comes to him more powerful."

When morning came, the father went into the forest again, climbed the hill, and shook the poles, calling his son out.

"Father," Opichi said as he emerged, shaking from the cold, "last night a beaver came to me. It taught me a song."

"That is good," said the father. "You are doing well. You will gain ever more power if you stay longer."

"I will watch and wait," said the boy.

So it went for four more days. Each morning his father asked Opichi what he had seen. Each time the boy told of his experiences from the night before. Now hawk and wolf, bear and eagle had visited the boy. Each day Opichi looked thinner and weaker, but he agreed to stay and wait for an ever-greater vision to please his father.

At last, on the morning of the seventh day, Opichi's mother spoke to her husband. "Our son has waited long enough in the forest. I will go with you this morning, and we will bring him home."

Opichi's mother and father went together into the forest. The gentle breath of the Fawn, the warm south wind of spring, had blown during the night, and all the snow had melted away. As they climbed the hill, they heard a birdsong coming from above them. It was a song they had never heard before. It sounded almost like the name of their son.

Opi chi chi
Opi chi chi

When they reached the lodge, Opichi's father shook the poles. "My son," he said, "it is time to end your fast. It is time to come home."

There was no answer. Opichi's mother and father bent down to look into the small lean-to of hemlock boughs and saplings. As they did so, a bird came flying out. It was gray and black with a red chest.

Opi chi chi
Opi chi chi

So it sang as it perched on a branch above them. Then it spoke.

"My parents," said the bird, "you see me as I am now. The one who was your son is gone. You sent him out too early and asked him to wait for power too long. Now I will return each spring when the gentle breath of the Fawn comes to our land. My song will let people know it is the time for a boy to go on his dream fast. But your words must help to remind his parents not to make their son stay out too long."

Then, singing that song which was the name of their son, the robin flew off into the forest.

White Weasel
Abenaki

One day, as a hunter was walking through the forest, he heard the sound of a dog howling.

"Someone is in trouble," said the hunter, whose name was Wolverine. He followed the pitiful howling to an abandoned village and found the dog sitting in front of a small wigwam. As soon as it saw Wolverine, it wagged its tail and came over. Then the dog led the hunter inside the wigwam, where a little baby was tied to a cradleboard. The baby was thin and hungry, and his face was covered with scabs.

"Little one," Wolverine said, picking up the child, "I will take pity on you." Then, followed by the dog, he went back to his lodge and handed the baby to his wife, Fisher.

"I give you a child," Wolverine said. "He is starved and sick. He was abandoned to die."

"I am glad to have him," Fisher said. "I will cure him and he will grow strong. Tomorrow I will go out and name him after the first animal I see."

In the morning, Fisher went out into the forest. She had not walked far when a small animal came out of the bushes. It was a little weasel, the color of the newly fallen snow. It was quick in its movements and looked up at her without fear. "You have given my grandson his name," said Fisher. So the boy was named White Weasel.

Wolverine and Fisher cared well for their adopted grandson. They taught him all they knew of hunting and medicine and told him how he was found abandoned.

Many seasons passed, and White Weasel became wiry and strong. He was a good hunter and knew how to use the healing plants of the forest. Finally the day came when he knew he had to leave his foster grandparents.

"Grandfather," he asked Wolverine, "are there other people in the world?"

"Yes," said Wolverine, "but they are far away to the north near the great water."

"I will go there," said White Weasel. "I must find my parents."

"Listen well," Fisher said. "Your parents left you to die. Only your dog, Bad Dog, stayed to watch over you and save your life. You will not know your parents, but your dog will know them. Follow him and he will guide you to them."

"Grandmother," White Weasel said, "I will do as you say. Now I need snowshoes, for I must go to the north."

So Grandmother Fisher made snowshoes from rawhide and ash wood, and White Weasel set out, following his dog.

The boy and his dog traveled north for many days. Then one morning as they were starting out, White Weasel heard the sound of weeping. He looked down to the left of the trail and saw a small man who sat crying. He was one of the little people, the Mikumwesuk.

"Uncle," said White Weasel, "what is wrong?"

"My wife is sick," the little man said. "I know that she will die."

"My grandmother taught me medicine," said White Weasel. "I will help your wife."

Mikumwesu led him through the forest along a twisting path until they came to what looked like a pile of brush. As soon as they went inside, White Weasel saw it was a beautiful lodge. On a pile of rabbit skins was a little woman with a thin, pale face.

"I can cure your sickness," White Weasel said. He gathered herbs and made them into a tea. Mikumwesu's wife drank the tea, and by the morning she was well and strong.

"*Ktsi nidoba*, great friend," said Mikumwesu, "you saved my wife. I will go help you find what you seek." Then White Weasel and Mikumwesu set out together, following the dog. But when the sun was two hands high at midmorning, Mikumwesu stopped near a clearing.

"I must gather spruce gum," he said. He pulled gum from the trees around them, rolled it between his hands, and made six plugs. "Now," Mikumwesu said, "we must put these plugs into our ears. Soon we will need them."

The boy put the plugs into his ears and the ears of his dog. Then he followed Mikumwesu up a cliff. When they looked back toward the path they had left, they saw the trees shaking. Two huge Kiwakwes, the fierce giants of the North, came into the clearing, one from the east and one from the west. As White Weasel watched, the giant from the east threw a stone larger than a wigwam. It shattered when it struck the other giant's chest. Then the giant from the west pulled up a tall pine tree and swung it like a club. It splintered like a twig over the first giant's head. Their mouths were open as they fought, but White Weasel could hear nothing.

The Kiwakwes fought back and forth till the sun was in the middle of the sky. Finally the giant from the east threw the other to the ground and killed him. As White

Weasel and Mikumwesu watched, the Kiwakwe drank the blood of his defeated enemy, then went back into the woods to the east.

Mikumwesu waited a long time before he took the plugs of spruce gum from his ears. White Weasel did the same.

"Look around in the forest below," the little man said.

White Weasel looked. At first he saw nothing. Then he saw many animals—deer, bears, and others—lying dead.

"They were killed by the howling of the giants as they fought," Mikumwesu said. "If we had heard their terrible howls, we also would have died."

Once more they started north, following the little dog. After traveling for four days, Mikumwesu stopped them again.

"We are near the great water," Mikumwesu said. "Tomorrow you must send your small dog ahead to clear the path."

When the morning came, White Weasel said to his dog, "Bad Dog, danger is ahead of us. Go and clear our path so we can travel safely."

Wagging his tail, Bad Dog set out. He had not gone far when he came to two hemlock trees on either side of the trail. Beneath each tree, a huge snake was hidden. Bad Dog breathed in one, two, three, four times. With each breath, he became bigger. When he was taller than the trees, he grabbed one snake and then the other and shook them till they were dead. Then he breathed out one, two, three, four times and was small again.

Wagging his tail, Bad Dog set forth once more. Soon he came to two large stones, one on each side of the trail. Behind each stone, a great bear was hiding. Again Bad Dog breathed in four times and grew larger with each breath. With a growl, he leaped on the bears and killed each one with a single bite. Then, just as before, he breathed out four times and was small again.

When White Weasel's dog returned to him, the sun was four hands high.

"Bad Dog has done well," said Mikumwesu. "Now the trail is clear. Tomorrow you will reach the village of the people who killed your parents. All of the people in that village are bad. They have killed all the other people here in the North. They killed your parents and pretended to be your father and mother, but your dog would not let them enter your wigwam. So they left you there to die."

White Weasel and his dog went along the trail. They passed between two tall hemlock trees, and White Weasel saw many crows and jays eating something dead. They passed between two great stones, and White Weasel saw many ravens and foxes eating something dead. At last they came to a hill. Below them were the great water and a village on the shore. White Weasel followed his dog to the first wigwam in the village, where the dog stopped and growled.

"Wife," said a harsh voice from within, "hear me. Bad Dog has come."

White Weasel went to the door of the lodge. "*Kwe,*" he called. "Hello."

"*Kwe,*" the harsh voice called back from within. "Come inside."

White Weasel and his dog entered the lodge. A man and woman in beautiful clothing sat by the fire. They were very attractive, but the boy did not trust what he saw in their eyes.

"You have found our dog," said the woman. "Give him to us."

"Bad Dog is mine," said White Weasel. "He has protected me since I was a small, sick baby."

The two people looked long and hard at White Weasel. "You are our son," said the man. "Bad Dog carried you off into the forest a long time ago. We are glad to see you. Come and meet the people of our village."

The man who pretended to be White Weasel's father led them out of the lodge. There, by the door, stood Mikumwesu.

"Who is this ugly little man?" said the woman who pretended to be White Weasel's mother.

"You should not insult me," said Mikumwesu. "Soon your village will be covered with sumac trees." The sumacs were the first trees to grow in a deserted village, and Mikumwesu's words were a warning to these people that they would be destroyed.

Many other people began to come out of their lodges. They made fun of White Weasel and Mikumwesu, but the boy and the little man ignored their words.

"My dear son," said the man, "we are glad you have returned. Now we want to play with you. Do you like to wrestle?"

"Yes," said White Weasel, "I am a good wrestler."

"Great friend," said Mikumwesu, reaching into his pouch and drawing the boy aside, "put on these white moccasins. Then you will always land on your feet."

White Weasel put on the moccasins and followed the one who pretended to be his father till they arrived at a big wigwam on a stone ledge near the water. A huge man came out of that wigwam.

"You will wrestle with me," said the big man.

"Grab hold and try to throw me," said White Weasel.

The big man grabbed the boy, lifted him high, and threw him down to break his bones on the rocks. But White Weasel landed lightly on his feet.

"This is fun," said the boy. "Throw me again."

The big man became very angry and threw White Weasel a second time, trying to break his head. Just as before, the boy landed on his feet. Four times the big man tried to kill White Weasel, and four times he failed. Then White Weasel held up his hands.

"Now it is my turn," he said. He lifted the big man up and threw him down so hard that the big man could not move.

"This game is good," said White Weasel. "Who will wrestle me next?" But no one came forward.

The two who pretended to be his parents stood to one side, talking.

"My son," said the man, "it is late. Tomorrow we will play a better game. We will go out to the little island at dawn and play ball with you."

"Come and spend the night in our lodge," said the woman.

"No," said the boy, "I am used to sleeping in the forest."

As White Weasel and Mikumwesu walked toward the forest, the man who pretended to be White Weasel's father called to the dog. "Bad Dog," he said, "come to me." But White Weasel's dog only growled and followed his master into the forest, where White Weasel and Mikumwesu built a fire and made camp.

That night there were many strange sounds in the forest around them. Four times the noises came very close. Each time, Bad Dog ran growling into the darkness and returned with blood on his teeth.

At dawn White Weasel and Mikumwesu went back to the village. The people of the village were waiting. Many of them were limping and had wounds on their arms and legs.

"My son," said the man who pretended to be White Weasel's father, "ride with me in our canoe."

Mikumwesu took White Weasel aside. "They will drown you if you ride with them. I will make a better canoe." The little man went down to the shore to a big white stone. He turned it over and shaped it into a canoe, then pushed it out onto the water. When he got inside, there was a paddle in his hands. White Weasel and Bad Dog climbed in with him, and the people of the village followed in their canoes of birch bark. Soon they reached the little island.

"Our ball field is on the other side of this island," said the one who pretended to be White Weasel's father. "Leave your dog here. No dogs can come to our ball field."

Again Mikumwesu spoke softly to White Weasel. "Great friend, these bad people will kill you when you reach the other side. Follow them till you reach the middle of the island, then turn around and run back here as quick as you can."

White Weasel set out, always staying a little behind the people of the village as they laughed and joked.

"This boy will never see another ball game better than ours," they said.

White Weasel kept stopping to tie one moccasin string and then the other. When the bad people were far ahead, he turned and ran as quick as he could back to the canoe and jumped in. He and Mikumwesu began to paddle.

"Look back," said the little man.

White Weasel looked back. The bad people were running down to their canoes. They no longer were disguised as human beings. Now he could see they were monsters.

Mikumwesu stood in the canoe and faced north.

"Grandfather," he called, "blow this island away."

Then a great wind came out of the north. It blew and it blew. When it stopped blowing, the island and the bad people were gone and were never seen again.

When they reached the mainland, Mikumwesu spoke to White Weasel.

"Great friend," he said, "I must go back to my wife. Return to your grandparents. Good things will happen now that the bad people have been swept away."

White Weasel and his dog walked south for many days. When they reached home, things were not as before. There were many lodges and many people who welcomed him and took him to the lodge of his grandparents.

"Grandson," said Fisher, "you have become a tall man."

"Grandson," said Wolverine, "now that the bad ones are gone and their village grown over with sumacs, your relatives have returned."

So White Weasel was reunited with his people. He became their chief and all went well for many years, and it was still going well when I left them.

Racing the Great Bear
Iroquois

Ne *onendji*. Hear my story, which happened long ago. For many generations, the five nations of the Haudenosaunee, the People of the Longhouse, had been at war with one another. No one could say how the wars began, but each time a man of one nation was killed, his relatives sought revenge in the blood feud, and so the fighting continued. Then the Creator took pity on his people and sent a messenger of peace. The Peacemaker traveled from nation to nation, convincing the people of the Five Nations—the Mohawk, the Oneida, the Onondaga, the Cayuga, and the Seneca— that it was wrong for brothers to kill one another. It was not easy, but finally the nations agreed and the Great Peace began. Most welcomed that peace, though there were some beings with bad hearts who wished to see the return of war.

One day, not long after the Great Peace had been established, some young men in a Seneca village decided they would pay a visit to the Onondaga people.

"It is safe now to walk the trail between our nations," the young men said. "We will return after the sun has risen and set seven times."

Then they set out. They walked toward the east until they were lost from sight in the hills. But many more than seven days passed, and those young men never returned. Now another group of young men left, wanting to find out where their friends had gone. They, too, did not return.

The people grew worried. Parties were sent out to look for the vanished young men, but no sign was found. And the searchers who went too far into the hills did not return, either.

The old chief of the village thought long and hard. He asked the clan mothers, those wise women whose job it was to choose the chiefs and give them good advice, what should be done.

"We must find someone brave enough to face whatever danger is out there," the clan mothers said.

So the old chief called the whole village to a council meeting. He held up a white strand of wampum beads made from quahog clamshells as he spoke.

"Hear me," he said. "I am of two minds about what has happened to our people. It may be that the Onondaga have broken the peace and captured them. It may be there is something with an evil mind that wishes to destroy this new peace and so has killed our people. Now someone must go and find out. Who is brave enough? Who will come and take this wampum from my hand?"

Many men were gathered in that council. Some were known to speak of themselves as brave warriors. Still, though they muttered to one another, no man stepped forward to take the strand of wampum. The old chief began to walk about the circle, holding the wampum in front of each man in turn. But each man only lowered his eyes to the ground. No man lifted his hand to take the wampum.

Just outside the circle stood a boy who had not yet become a man. His parents were dead, and he lived with his grandmother in her old lodge at the edge of the village. His clothing was always torn and his face dirty because his grandmother was too old to care for him as a mother would. The other young men made fun of him, and as a joke they called him Swift Runner—even though no one had ever seen him run and it was thought that he was weak and lazy. All he ever seemed to do was play with his little dog or sit by the fire and listen when the old people were talking.

"Our chief has forgotten our greatest warrior," one of the young men said to another, tilting his head toward Swift Runner.

"*Nyoh*," the other young man said, laughing. "Yes. Why does he not offer the wampum to Swift Runner?"

The chief looked around the circle of men, and the laughing stopped. He walked out of the circle to the place where the small boy in torn clothes stood. He held out the wampum and Swift Runner took it without hesitating.

"I accept this," Swift Runner said. "It is right that I be the one to face the danger. In the eyes of the people I am worthless, so if I do not return, it will not matter. I will leave when the sun rises tomorrow."

When Swift Runner arrived home at his grandmother's lodge, the old woman was waiting for him.

"Grandson," she said, "I know what you have done. The people of this village no longer remember, but your father was a great warrior. Our family is a family that has power."

Then she reached up into the rafters and took down a heavy bow. It was blackened with smoke and seemed so thick that no man could bend it.

"If you can string this bow, Grandson," the old woman said, "you are ready to face whatever waits for you on the trail."

Swift Runner took the bow. It was as thick as a man's wrist, but he bent it with ease and strung it.

"Wah-hah!" said his grandmother. "You are the one I knew you would grow up to be. Now you must sleep. At dawn we will make you ready for your journey."

It was not easy for Swift Runner to sleep, but when he woke the next morning, he felt strong and clear-headed. His grandmother was sitting by the fire with a cap in her hand.

"This was your grandfather's cap," she said. "I have sewed four hummingbird feathers on it. It will make your feet more swift."

Swift Runner took the cap and placed it on his head.

His grandmother held up four pairs of moccasins. "Carry these tied to your waist. When one pair wears out, throw them aside and put on the next pair."

Swift Runner took the moccasins and tied them to his belt.

Next his grandmother picked up a small pouch. "In this pouch is cornmeal mixed with maple sugar," she said. "It is the only food you will need as you travel. It will give you strength when you eat it each evening."

Swift Runner took the pouch and hung it from his belt by the moccasins.

"The last thing I must give you," said the old woman, "is this advice. Pay close attention to your little dog. You have treated him well and so he is your great friend. He is small, but his eyes and nose are keen. Keep him always in front of you. He will warn you of danger before it can strike you."

Then Swift Runner set out on his journey. His little dog stayed ahead of him, sniffing the air and sniffing the ground. By the time the sun was in the middle of the sky, they were far from the village. The trail passed through deep woods, and it seemed to the boy as if something was following them among the trees. But he could see nothing in the thick brush.

The trail curved toward the left, and the boy felt even more the presence of something watching. Suddenly his little dog ran into the brush at the side of the trail, barking loudly. There were the sounds of tree limbs breaking and heavy feet running. Then out of the forest came a Nyagwahe, a monster bear. Its great teeth were as long as a man's arm. It was twice as tall as a moose. Close at its heels was Swift Runner's little dog.

"I see you," Swift Runner shouted. "I am after you. You cannot escape me."

Swift Runner had learned those words by listening to the stories the old people told. They were the very words a monster bear speaks when it attacks, words that terrify anyone who hears them. On hearing those words, the great bear turned and fled from the boy.

"You cannot escape me," Swift Runner shouted again. Then he ran after the bear.

The Nyagwahe turned toward the east, with Swift Runner and his dog close behind. It left the trail and plowed through the thick forest, breaking down great trees and leaving a path of destruction like that of a whirlwind. It ran up the tallest hills and down through the swamps, but the boy and the dog stayed at its heels. They ran past a great cave in the rocks. All around the cave were the bones of people the bear had caught and eaten.

"My relatives," Swift Runner called as he passed the cave, "I will not forget you. I am after the one who killed you. He will not escape me."

Throughout the day, the boy and his dog chased the great bear, growing closer bit by bit. At last, as the sun began to set, Swift Runner stopped at the head of a small valley and called his small dog to him.

"We will rest here for the night," the boy said. He took off his first pair of moccasins, whose soles were worn away to nothing. He threw them aside and put on a new pair. Swift Runner made a fire and sat beside it with his dog. Then he took out the pouch of cornmeal and maple sugar, sharing his food with his dog.

"Nothing will harm us," Swift Runner said. "Nothing can come close to our fire." He lay down and slept.

In the middle of the night, he was awakened by the growling of his dog. He sat up with his back to the fire and looked into the darkness. There, just outside the circle of light made by the flames, stood a dark figure that looked like a tall man. Its eyes glowed green.

"I am Nyagwahe," said the figure. "This is my human shape. Why do you pursue me?"

"You cannot escape me," Swift Runner said. "I chase you because you killed my people. I will not stop until I catch you and kill you."

The figure faded back into the darkness.

"You cannot escape me," Swift Runner said again. Then he patted his small dog and went to sleep.

As soon as the first light of the new day appeared, Swift Runner rose. He and his small dog took the trail. It was easy to follow the monster's path, for trees were uprooted and the earth torn by its great paws. They ran all through the morning. When the sun was in the middle of the sky, they reached the head of another valley. At the other end they saw the great bear running toward the east. Swift Runner pulled off his second pair of moccasins, whose soles were worn away to nothing. He put on his third pair and began to run again.

All through that day, they kept the Nyagwahe in sight, drawing closer bit by bit. When the sun began to set, Swift Runner stopped to make camp. He took off the third pair of moccasins, whose soles were worn away to nothing, and put on the last pair.

"Tomorrow," he said to his small dog, "we will catch the monster and kill it." He reached for his pouch of cornmeal and maple sugar, but when he opened it, he found it filled with worms. The magic of the Nyagwahe had done this. Swift Runner poured out the pouch and said in a loud voice, "You have spoiled our food, but it will not stop me. I am on your trail. You cannot escape me."

That night, once again, he was awakened by the growling of his dog. A dark figure stood just outside the circle of light. It looked smaller than the night before, and the glow of its eyes was weak.

"I am Nyagwahe," the dark figure said. "Why do you pursue me?"

"You cannot escape me," Swift Runner said. "I am on your trail. You killed my people. You threatened the Great Peace. I will not rest until I catch you."

"Hear me," said the Nyagwahe. "I see your power is greater than mine. Do not kill me. When you catch me, take my great teeth. They are my power, and you can use them for healing. Spare my life and I will go far to the north and never again bother the People of the Longhouse."

"You cannot escape me," Swift Runner said. "I am on your trail."

The dark figure faded back into the darkness, and Swift Runner sat for a long time, looking into the night.

At the first light of day, the boy and his dog took the

trail. They had not gone far when they saw the Nyag-wahe ahead of them. Its sides puffed in and out as it ran. The trail was beside a big lake with many alder trees close to the water. As the great bear ran past, the leaves were torn from the trees. Fast as the bear went, the boy and his dog came closer, bit by bit. At last, when the sun was in the middle of the sky, the giant bear could run no longer. It fell heavily to the earth, panting so hard that it stirred up clouds of dust.

Swift Runner unslung his grandfather's bow and notched an arrow to the sinewy string.

"Shoot for my heart," said the Nyagwahe. "Aim well. If you cannot kill me with one arrow, I will take your life."

"No," Swift Runner said. "I have listened to the stories of my elders. Your only weak spot is the sole of your foot. Hold up your foot and I will kill you."

The great bear shook with fear. "You have defeated me," it pleaded. "Spare my life and I will leave forever."

"You must give me your great teeth," Swift Runner said. "Then you must leave and never bother the People of the Longhouse again."

"I shall do as you say," said the Nyagwahe. "Take my great teeth."

Swift Runner lowered his bow. He stepped forward and pulled out the great bear's teeth. It rose to its feet and walked to the north, growing smaller as it went. It went over the hill and was gone.

Carrying the teeth of the Nyagwahe over his shoulder, Swift Runner turned back to the west, his dog at his side. He walked for three moons before he reached the place where the bones of his people were piled in front of the monster's empty cave. He collected those bones and walked around them four times. "Now," he said, "I must do something to make my people wake up." He went to a big hickory tree and began to push it over so that it would fall on the pile of bones.

"My people," he shouted, "get up quickly or this tree will land on you."

The bones of the people who had been killed all came together and jumped up, alive again and covered with flesh. They were filled with joy and gathered around Swift Runner.

"Great one," they said, "who are you?"

"I am Swift Runner," he said.

"How can that be?" one of the men said. "Swift Runner is a skinny little boy. You are a tall, strong man."

Swift Runner looked at himself and saw that it was so. He was taller than the tallest man, and his little dog was bigger than a wolf.

"I am Swift Runner," he said. "I was that boy and I am the man you see before you."

Then Swift Runner led his people back to the village. He carried with him the teeth of the Nyagwahe, and those who saw what he carried rejoiced. The trails were safe again, and the Great Peace would not be broken. Swift Runner went to his grandmother's lodge and embraced her.

"Grandson," she said, "you are now the man I knew you would grow up to be. Remember to use your power to help the people."

So it was that Swift Runner ran with the great bear and won the race. Throughout his long life, he used the teeth of the Nyagwahe to heal the sick, and he worked always to keep the Great Peace.

Da neho. I am finished.

Granny Squannit and the
Bad Young Man
Wampanoag

Long ago, Tooquahmi Squannit lived in a cave near the sand dunes at Cummaquid. Granny Squannit was an old, old woman. She was short and strong, and she wore her long black hair over her face so that only her mouth could be seen. She avoided other people most of the time and knew a great deal about medicine. Even though Granny Squannit lived away from the village at Nauset, she always seemed to know all of the things that were going on with the people. She was especially interested in the children. If a child misbehaved, she might appear suddenly in front of that child to frighten him. It was said that any child who had seen Granny Squannit was always good after that.

In those days, when a boy reached a certain age, it was the custom for him to go through a special initiation to prepare himself to become a man. That boy would be blindfolded and taken out deep into the forest by his uncle to a place where he was expected to stay for three moons. He was given nothing to help take care of himself. While he was gone he would have to build his own shelter and gather his own food. The boy was supposed to think deeply about the responsibility of being a man and caring for the people. This vigil in the forest was not an easy thing to do, but every boy who wished to become a man would do it.

One boy, however, refused to do as his elders suggested. When the time came for him to go alone into the forest, he said no. This boy always thought of himself first and not of others. He would not listen to advice from others. He showed no respect to his elders, even his own grandparents. It seemed as if a bad spirit had gotten into his heart, and there was no way to stop his bad behavior. His father spoke to him, but the boy did not change. His uncle spoke to him, but the boy ignored him. His grandfather spoke to him, but the boy paid no attention. Even the sachem, the old chief of the village, spoke to the boy, but it had no effect. In fact, if that boy was not watched every minute, he would destroy things.

"Where is our son?" his father asked one day.

"I do not know," his mother said, "but I smell something burning."

"Ah-ah! He has made a fire behind the lodge and is burning my arrows!"

The boy was taken to the *pauwau*, the wise old man who was able to cure diseases of the spirit and see deep into the heart of any sickness. The old man looked into the boy's face. He tried his strongest medicines, but they did not touch the badness that held on to the boy's heart. As soon as the *pauwau* turned his back, the boy grabbed the old man's wampum belts and ran down and threw them over the cliff into the ocean.

"There is nothing I can do," the *pauwau* said. "He is a bad young man."

And so that became the boy's name among the people: Bad Young Man. From that time on, no one called him by any other name.

One day, Bad Young Man followed some of the younger children down to the river. As soon as they got there, he began to push them into the water. But as he was doing this, a canoe came up the river. Even though the person in the canoe was not paddling, it cut its way swiftly upstream. And the person in the canoe was Granny Squannit, her long black hair over her face.

The other children climbed up onto the bank and ran, but Bad Young Man stood there in the water, unable to move. Granny Squannit's canoe came right up to him. Then the old woman reached out her arm and yanked him into the canoe. The canoe turned around and went swiftly down the river. Soon it was close to the ocean, near Cummaquid where the sand dunes rose. Granny Squannit pulled her canoe up onto the sand and then yanked Bad Young Man out of the canoe. She held him so hard by the arm that he could not pull away. She took him straight into her cave and sat him down.

Bad Young Man wanted to run away, but he could not move. Granny Squannit came to him with a bowl of green soup in her hand. She gave it to Bad Young Man, and even though he did not want to, he drank it all. And he fell asleep.

When he woke up, four days had passed. He looked around the cave. Where was the old woman who had brought him here? Then he saw Granny Squannit. She was lying across the mouth of the cave and she seemed to be asleep, her long black hair over her face.

If I am very quiet, he thought, I can sneak out and get away from her.

Carefully, quietly, he crawled toward the entrance of the cave. Carefully, quietly, he stepped over the old woman as she slept. But as he was about to leave, he became curious. No one had ever seen Granny Squannit's face. Bad Young Man turned back, leaned over, and pushed the hair away from the old woman's face so he could see what she really looked like. There, staring up at him was—not two eyes, but one! One huge, wide-open eye was there in the center of Granny Squannit's face. It seemed as if that eye were looking straight into the center of his spirit. The boy shouted and fell back against the wall of the cave.

Granny Squannit stood up. She could see that the badness had been frightened out of the boy. She pushed the hair in front of her face and took him by the arm, gently this time, to lead him back into the cave. She took out a deerskin pouch, placed roots and other medicine plants into it, and sewed it shut. Then she gave it to the boy.

"Wear this about your neck," Granny Squannit said. "It will remind you to keep goodness in your heart."

The boy did as she said. He returned to his people and was a bad young man no longer. Before long, he gained a new name. He became known as High Eagle. High Eagle respected his elders and did things with other people in mind. He continued to do good things and gained more respect, until one day High Eagle became Grand Sachem of his people.

THE SOUTHEAST

Perhaps more than those of people in any other section of North America, the lives of the Native peoples of the Southeast were disrupted by the coming of the Europeans. The Cherokee and Creek peoples were among the five nations that became known as the Five Civilized Tribes for their outward adoption of European ways. Despite the removal of most of the Cherokee and Creek peoples to Oklahoma, their cultures have shown great resilience. Farther to the west, at the southeastern edge of the plains, the Caddo and Osage peoples also found themselves forced to relocate to Oklahoma.

As a result of these forced migrations, the Native peoples of the Southeast, including those who have managed to remain in their original homelands, are often overlooked. This is a great shame, for they have not disappeared and—as the following stories show—they still have much to teach us all.

The ecological balance of things is important in

Native American traditions. If people behave correctly, nature will provide all that is needed. The Cherokee legend "How the Game Animals Were Set Free," one story exemplifying this belief, is both humorous and instructive. Learning in Native American cultures is usually through experience. Instead of being told how to behave, a child is allowed to make mistakes and then learns from the consequences.

On the other hand, that kind of freedom also permits a child to discover his or her own power. In the Caddo tale "The Wild Boy," the twins become powerful beings through their quest. As is the case in many Native stories, a wise parent lets the natural world teach the lesson through experience.

The highest ideal in these cultures, and in most of the cultures of Native North America, is not to achieve personal wealth but to gain the knowledge and the power that will enable individuals to serve their people. A high degree of individual freedom carries with it an equally large responsibility to the community. In the Creek story "The Underwater Lodge," Blue Fox fails to discharge properly his duty to his father. He risks his life in the domain of the fearful tie-snakes until he understands the meaning of freedom and responsibility.

The Osage also believed in living in harmony with nature. They were among the tallest of the people of the southeastern plains, yet they saw that they were small compared with the land around them and the greatness of Wah-Kon-Tah, the Great Mystery. So they called themselves the Little Ones.

The Osage divided themselves into two groups, the Honga (the People of the Earth) and the Tzi-sho (the

People of the Sky). Each of the many Osage clans was guided by the nonhuman beings around it—a plant, an animal, or even a star. "The Wisdom of the Willow Tree" is one such story of how a new symbol of wisdom and strength was given to a young man of the Earth People.

How the Game Animals Were Set Free
Cherokee

Long ago, at the foot of Looking-Glass Mountain, there lived a hunter named Kanati and his two sons, First Boy and Inage Utasuhi'. Inage Utasuhi', whose name meant "The Boy Who Grew Up Wild," was always getting himself and his brother into trouble.

Each day Kanati, whose name meant "The Lucky Hunter," would go out to get game for them to eat, and each day he was successful. First Boy and Inage Utasuhi' would stay behind and play hunting games together.

"Take us with you," Inage Utasuhi' would ask each day, but Kanati refused.

"You are not yet old enough to hunt. If you are not ready and you try to hunt, then bad things may happen. If you are not serious when you hunt, bad things will happen. When you are ready, I will take you with me."

The boys listened at first, but one morning when Kanati left the lodge, Inage Utasuhi' spoke to his brother. "Let us follow our father and watch what he does. How else can we learn to be men?"

The two boys set out, following their father but keeping back so he would not see them. Before long, Kanati came to a hollow tree. The boys could not see what he was doing.

"I will go closer," said Inage Utasuhi'. Then he changed himself into a small bird and flew to a branch of the hollow tree.

Kanati reached into the tree and pulled out a bundle covered in deerskin. When he unwrapped it, Inage Utasuhi' could see that there was something strange inside. It was a long, bent stick with a piece of strong cord made of milkweed fibers fastened from one end of it to the other. Then Kanati placed the deerskin wrappings in the hollow tree and began to walk. As he walked, he plucked the string and it made a humming sound.

Inage Utasuhi' flew back to First Boy and turned into a human again.

"I do not know what our father is doing," the wild boy said. "But if we wish to learn how to hunt, we must follow him and watch."

So the boys continued to follow Kanati. Soon he came to a swampy place where many reeds grew. Before their father went in among the reeds, Inage Utasuhi' spoke to his brother.

"Wait here," he said. "I will go and see what he does." Then the wild boy changed himself into a downy feather, floated through the wind, and landed unseen on Kanati's shoulder. In the shape of the downy feather, the wild boy watched closely as Kanati selected and cut the straightest reed. He reached into his pouch and took out a goose feather. He split it with his flint knife and then tied it with sinew to the reed. He cut a notch in one end of the reed and sharpened the other end. Then Kanati took the long, feathered reed and fitted it to the string of the bent stick he carried.

When Kanati returned from the reeds, the wind blew the downy feather off his shoulder. It floated back and forth in the air as the hunter walked away, and then, as soon as it touched the ground, turned into Inage Utasuhi'.

First Boy came out of the bushes where he had been hiding and joined his brother.

"We are learning a great deal," the wild boy said. "Let us continue to follow and see what our father does."

Before long, Kanati came to the side of Looking-Glass

Mountain. There was a cave, blocked by a big stone. Kanati rolled the stone away from the mouth of the cave, and a big deer came running out. Kanati raised the bow and shot his arrow, killing the deer. Then he rolled the stone in front of the cave, picked up his deer, and headed toward home.

"If we want to be men," Inage Utasuhi' said, "we must do as our father did."

So the two boys went back and cut saplings to make bows. They made cordage from milkweed fibers and strung their bows. They went into the reeds and cut the straightest ones. Then each of the boys made seven arrows.

"Now we are ready to hunt," said Inage Utasuhi'. He led his brother to the cave, and together they rolled away the stone. Immediately a big deer ran out. It came out so fast that the boys were too surprised to shoot. The wild boy struck at it with one of the arrows in his hand, but he only hit the deer's tail, knocking it straight up. The deer bounded off into the forest with the white of its tail showing above its back.

"Oho, brother, did you see that?" Inage Utasuhi' said, laughing. "See if you can do the same."

Another deer ran out and First Boy struck at its tail with his arrow. As soon as he knocked the tail, it stood straight up and stayed there as the deer ran away. Both boys laughed. This was great fun. For a long time, they took turns striking at each deer as it ran out, until all the deer had left the cave. Ever since then, all deer have tails that stick straight up when they run.

Other game animals began to come out of the cave. The boys watched them. Soon, so many were running out that Inage Utasuhi' and First Boy became afraid.

They tried to move the stone back, but the animals were too fast and too many. Rabbits and raccoons and squirrels and possums and all of the four-legged animals came out while the boys just watched. Then birds flew out in great numbers. There were turkeys and grouse and pigeons and all the other birds that people hunted. They came out in flocks so large, they darkened the sky and their wings were like the rumble of thunder. Now the boys grew frightened, but they could not roll the stone into the mouth of the cave.

Back in his lodge, Kanati heard the rumbling sound. He looked up and saw the sky was dark with birds.

"Oho," he said, "what are my bad boys doing?" He left the lodge quickly and hurried to the cave. Fast as Kanati ran, he was not fast enough. By the time he came to the place where he had kept the game animals and the birds, all of them had escaped. The two boys were still standing there, watching.

Kanati said nothing. But he knew that his boys needed to be punished for their deed. He went into the cave and brought out four clay pots. Putting them down, he knocked the lid off each one. Biting insects came flying out and landed on the two boys. Though Inage Utasuhi' and First Boy swatted and jumped, they could not rid themselves of the fleas and flies, the gnats and mosquitoes. At last Kanati thought they had been punished enough. He brushed the insects off the boys. But the insects did not go back into the pots. They went out and spread all over the world. And to this day, there are still fleas and flies and gnats and mosquitoes.

"You have not done well," Kanati said to the boys. "It will no longer be easy for us to hunt. Had you done as I said and waited until you were ready, the game animals would not have been freed. A hunter must always be serious and show respect for the animals. You were not serious as you hunted, and so all the game animals escaped. You have learned how to make bows and arrows, and they will be needed from now on. No longer can we be sure that we will bring home game animals to eat. Now we will have to work hard to hunt the animals, and even then we cannot be sure of success."

And so, because of what Kanati's sons did back then, it is still that way to this day.

The Wild Boy
Caddo

There was a hunter who lived with his wife and their son, a boy twelve winters old, in a lodge near a stream deep in the woods. Because this hunter was wise in the ways of healing and plants, he was called Medicine Person. Each day, when he came home with the game he had killed, his wife would take it down to the stream to wash the blood away.

One day, when the hunter returned carrying a large deer, his wife was gone. Their son was sitting in the back of the lodge. He looked frightened and tired.

"Where is your mother?" Medicine Person said.

"I do not know," Lodge Boy answered. "She went to the spring to get water, and I heard a scream and a terrible noise. I ran there and called for her many times, but she did not return."

Medicine Person and Lodge Boy searched a long time for her. All they could find were some of her torn clothes and the tracks of a large animal leading away to the west. With great sorrow, the hunter accepted that his wife was dead. Together he and his son built a fire and kept it burning for six days as they sat beside it in mourning. On the seventh day, Medicine Person went hunting again.

"My son," Medicine Person said as he left, "do not go far from our lodge when I am away."

"Can I go down to the stream and play?" the boy asked.

"Yes," Medicine Person said, "but go no farther than that."

Each day for many days after that, when Medicine Person came home, he found his son waiting for him.

One evening, however, Medicine Person returned from hunting by a different trail than the one he usually took. When he reached the lodge, his son was not there. But as he listened carefully, he heard the sound of voices coming from the direction of the stream. Medicine Person did not take the trail but crept down to the stream through the brush. When he looked out, he saw his son and another boy talking and playing. The other boy was about his son's size and resembled him, except that the other boy had long, tangled hair and a long nose. As soon as Medicine Person stepped out of his hiding place, the other boy leaped into the stream and was gone.

"Who are you playing with?" Medicine Person asked his son. "Who are his parents and where does he live?"

"Father," Lodge Boy said, "my friend does not have a name, and he lives in the forest. He says that his mother is my mother, but she came here to the stream and threw him away."

As soon as he heard those words, Medicine Person understood. This wild boy had sprung from the blood of the deer that his wife always washed in the stream.

"My son," Medicine Person said, "we must bring your brother into our lodge. It is not right that he should have to live alone in the forest."

"That will not be easy, Father. I have tried to bring him to our lodge before, but he says he must remain in the forest and not be tamed. He always runs away when he hears you coming home because he says that you will make him live like a human being."

"Tomorrow," Medicine Person said, "I will only pretend to go hunting. I will turn myself into a cricket and hide here by the side of the lodge. Bring your brother close and I will jump out and grab him."

The next day Medicine Person turned himself into a cricket and hid while Lodge Boy went down to the stream. Soon the boy came back up the trail with his brother beside him. But as soon as Wild Boy saw the cricket by the side of the lodge, he stopped.

"Who is that man hiding behind the lodge?" Wild Boy asked. Then he turned and ran away.

The next day Medicine Person tried again. "I will make myself into a stick and hide in the roof of the lodge. Bring your brother close and I will catch him."

Just as before, Wild Boy came within sight of the lodge and stopped. "Who is that man hiding in the roof?" he asked, looking at the stick. Then he ran away.

Each day Medicine Person tried another hiding place. Each day Wild Boy saw him and ran away. Finally, on the night before the seventh day, Medicine Person left Lodge Boy by their lodge and went to a little clearing in the forest. At the edge of the clearing, he made a small shelter covered with grass and leaves so that it could not easily be seen. Then he returned to their lodge and spoke to his son.

"Tomorrow we must catch your brother, for I will have used up all of my powers. You must do as I say. Take Wild Boy to the clearing west of our lodge. I will leave a fire burning there. Sit him by the fire and tell him that you wish to comb out his hair. As you do so, knot his hair four times and hold on to it and call me."

This time Medicine Person did not let Lodge Boy know where he was going to hide. Soon, from his hiding place, he heard the sound of the boys approaching.

"Brother," Lodge Boy said, "let me comb the tangles out of your hair."

Wild Boy looked around but could see no one. He sat

down by the fire and turned his back to his brother. As soon as Lodge Boy had made four knots in the hair of Wild Boy, he held on and called out, "Father, we are ready."

Then Medicine Person jumped out of the fire where he had been hiding and grabbed hold of Wild Boy. He took him to the little shelter covered with grass and leaves and placed him and his brother inside it for six days. On the seventh day, he brought the boys out. Lodge Boy washed his brother clean, and Medicine Person took his knife and cut off the long end of Wild Boy's nose. The two boys looked like twins.

Medicine Person said to Wild Boy, "You have been playing with my son and calling him your brother. Now you are brothers indeed. Stay in our lodge and play with him while I am gone."

Medicine Person went off to hunt. But before he left, he told his boys not to go toward the west, for there were giant squirrels there that killed and ate children.

However, even though he now looked like his brother, it was still Wild Boy's nature to do things his own way. As soon as Medicine Person was out of sight, Wild Boy picked up his bow and arrows.

"Brother," he said, "let us walk toward the west."

The two brothers walked and walked until they came to a place in the forest where the trees were very tall. In one of the trees was a big hollow and, in that hollow, the giant squirrels lived.

"We will stay far away from the tree, and the giant squirrels will not be able to reach us," Wild Boy said. But even as he spoke, one of the giant squirrels poked out its head and saw the boys. It opened its mouth and a long tongue, longer than the tongue of a frog, flicked out and caught Lodge Boy. Before Wild Boy could do anything, the giant squirrel had swallowed his brother and disappeared back into the tree. Without saying anything, Wild Boy turned and walked home. When he went into the lodge, his father was there, home from hunting.

"Where is your brother?" Medicine Person asked.

"He is waiting for me in the forest. We are making arrows. I came home to get fire so that we could heat the shafts to straighten them," Wild Boy answered. He picked up a burning brand from the fire and left.

When he reached the place in the forest where the tall trees grew and the giant squirrels lived, Wild Boy made a big fire using the burning brand. He gathered red stones and placed them in the fire until they were white with heat.

Then he picked up the stones with peeled green branches and threw them into the hollow tree. Smoke began to pour out of the tree. Finally the giant squirrel came crawling from the hole and fell dead on the ground. Wild Boy turned it over and cut open its stomach. Out crawled Lodge Boy, unharmed.

"Do not tell our father what happened," Wild Boy said. "If he finds out, he will not let us play anymore."

"Brother, you are right," Lodge Boy said. Then the brothers went back home. When they arrived at the lodge, Medicine Person was waiting for them but said nothing. So the two brothers were able to continue to play together.

The next day, Medicine Person spoke to his sons. "While I am gone, stay close to the lodge. Do not go to the west, for that is where the ones who eat human beings live. They are the ones who killed your mother."

The two boys waited until their father had left and then began to play the game of shooting at the hoop. They had made a hoop of elm bark, and each boy would take a turn rolling it while the other boy shot at it, trying to stop it with his arrows.

Wild Boy, however, soon tired of the game. He made two magical arrows, one black and one blue, and gave them to his brother.

"Use these arrows for our game," he said. Then Wild Boy rolled the hoop. Each time the hoop was rolled, Lodge Boy shot one of the magic arrows and struck the hoop, stopping it.

"Roll it faster, brother," Lodge Boy said. "This is too easy."

Wild Boy blew on the hoop to fill it, too, with magic power. He rolled the hoop as hard as he could. It went past Lodge Boy so fast that he did not shoot, and it rolled toward the western horizon, where it seemed to go up into the sky as it went out of sight.

"We have lost our hoop," Lodge Boy said sadly.

"Do not worry, brother," Wild Boy said. "We will be able to go where it has gone and find it." He picked up a buffalo-calf robe that Medicine Person had tanned, draped it over his shoulders, and began to walk.

The two boys walked together toward the horizon. They walked for a long time, following the track made by the hoop as it rolled across the ground. When it was midday, Wild Boy stopped, for the track of the hoop had ended.

"Here is the place where our hoop has gone up into the sky," he said. "Now I must go up and follow it." He reached into his pouch and brought out two nuts from the pecan tree. Placing one in the earth, he spoke a few words. Immediately a pecan tree burst up from the soil. It grew taller and taller, high into the sky.

"You must be ready to help me," Wild Boy said. "I am going to climb up to the top. Do not watch me as I climb, but continue always to look down at the earth. I will be gone a long time. You will know when I have reached the top, for my bones will begin to fall back to the ground. You must wait till all of them have fallen and gather them together. Cover them with this buffalo-calf robe. Shoot the blue arrow into the robe and call on me to stand up."

Wild Boy began to climb the tree. Up and up he went as Lodge Boy sat at the base of the tree, looking always at the ground. A long time passed, but Lodge Boy did not look up. Then a small bone fell on the ground beside him. More and more bones fell around him, until he was certain that all of Wild Boy's bones were there. He gathered the bones together, covered them with the robe, and drew back his arrow.

"Brother," he shouted, "stand up now!" He fired the blue arrow into the buffalo-calf robe, and when it struck, Wild Boy was standing there next to the robe. He was much the same as before, yet there was something different about him.

"Our Great Father has given me much power," Wild Boy said. "Now you must climb up, too, and you will be given power." He sat down by the big pecan tree and stared at the ground as Lodge Boy climbed. After a long time, Lodge Boy's bones fell from the tree. When they had all fallen, Wild Boy gathered them and covered them with the buffalo-calf robe. He drew back the blue arrow and shouted, "Get up, brother, or this arrow will strike you." As soon as his arrow struck the robe, Lodge Boy was standing there.

"Tell me," Wild Boy said, "what happened to you?"

"I climbed so high," Lodge Boy said, "that I reached the top of the tree. I could see nothing, and it seemed as if I were dreaming. Then the Great Sky Father touched me, and I watched as my bones fell toward the earth. I heard you call to me and I stood up."

"That is how it was with me," Wild Boy said. "You, too, have been given great power. Let me see what kind of power you have."

Lodge Boy opened his mouth and a great sound, the rolling of thunder, filled the air.

"You are Thunder Boy now," said Wild Boy. "Let me test my power." He opened his mouth and lightning came from it.

"You are Lightning Boy," his brother said. "But we must return to our lodge, for our father will be worried."

"No," Lightning Boy said, "first we must find the track of our hoop and locate it. When I was up in the sky, I could see the place where it was brought back down to the earth by the one who called it into the sky. The one who took the hoop is dangerous, but our power will protect us now." He put the buffalo-calf robe over his shoulders. "Let us go."

The two brothers set out again. Before they had gone far, they found the track of the hoop in the earth. They walked a long way until they came to a very wide lake. The brothers could see no way around it.

"We must cross over," Lightning Boy said. "My power tells me that our hoop is on the other side."

He reached into his pouch and pulled out the second pecan nut. As he planted it, he spoke a few words and again a tall pecan tree burst up from the earth. But as this tree grew, it began to curve until its top touched the ground on the other side of the lake. The boys crossed over this bridge and again found the track of their hoop. However, after they followed it a short way, the trail ended. There, coming toward them, was a figure that Thunder Boy thought was an old man. The old man smiled at Thunder Boy and held up the elm-bark hoop he was carrying.

"That is not really an old man," Lightning Boy said. "My power tells me he is the evil one who stole our hoop and means to kill us. Use your power, brother."

Thunder Boy opened his mouth and the sound of thunder split the air. The old man stopped coming toward them and turned to run. Lightning Boy opened his mouth and lightning shot out, striking the old man. As the lightning hit and killed him, they saw he was not an old man at all, but a being shaped like a human with long, sharp teeth and long, clawed hands. He was a Man-Eater. Beside his body was the elm-bark hoop.

"We must follow his tracks," Lightning Boy said. "His village is close to here." Then Lightning Boy used his power again. He bent over, and when he straightened up he looked like an old man, just as the Man-Eater had. Thunder Boy walked behind his brother as they followed the old man's trail back toward the lake. Before long they saw a village and what appeared to be many people standing in the center of the town. However, when Thunder Boy used his power, he could see that these beings, too, had long, sharp teeth and long, clawed fingers. They were Man-Eaters.

When they saw the old man coming into the village leading the boy, the Man-Eaters became excited.

"Our chief has brought food," they shouted.

Then Lightning Boy stood up straight and no longer looked like an old man. "Use your power," he said to his brother.

Thunder Boy opened his mouth and the sound of thunder rolled over the land, knocking all of those in the village to the ground. Lightning Boy opened his mouth and lightning flashed out, killing all the Man-Eaters.

"Let us look through the bones of the people they ate," said Lightning Boy. They began to rummage through the piles of bones scattered about the village. There were bones of humans of all shapes and sizes. Thunder Boy lifted up a bone from one pile off to the side of the others. As soon as he did so, he heard a familiar voice saying, "My son, I am glad you have found me."

"These are the bones of our mother!" Thunder Boy said excitedly.

Thunder Boy and Lightning Boy gathered together all of their mother's bones and covered them with the buffalo-calf robe.

"Mother," the boys shouted, "get up or these arrows will strike you!" Before the arrows pierced the skin, their mother stood there, alive and well.

"My sons," she said, "I have been sleeping too long." Then she embraced both the boys.

The three of them walked back toward the east where Medicine Person's lodge stood. When they reached the clearing, they saw that grass and small trees had grown all around the lodge, and there was no sign of life. Although it had seemed that their journey took only a single day, they had been gone for many years. They had been gone so long that their father thought them dead.

"Father," the boys called. "We have returned. Our mother is with us."

Then Medicine Person came out of his lodge. He looked old and tired, but when he saw his wife and his sons, the weight of the years lifted from him and he stood straight again.

For many years after, Medicine Person and his wife lived together happily with their sons. But when their parents finally died, Thunder Boy and Lightning Boy wished to stay no longer on the earth. They went up into the sky and there they remain. And, to this very day, when the two brothers look down from the clouds and see evil beings planning to harm their people, the voice of Thunder Boy may be heard as Lightning Boy's bolts flash through the sky.

The Underwater Lodge
Muskogee (Creek)

Long ago, the Muskogee people lived in the southern land of many rivers. There were many towns of the Muskogee, and one of the largest was the town of Koweta. One day, the chief of Koweta called his son, Blue Fox, to him. Blue Fox was a slender youth who had not yet been initiated into manhood. He loved and respected his father, but like all boys he also loved to play with his friends. Often when his father looked for him, he would be playing ball or running through the woods or swimming down at the river with his friends. His father hoped that his son would learn the importance of responsibility so that someday he, too, might be chosen to serve the people as their chief.

"My son," he said one morning, "you are young, but you are a good runner. I wish you to take a message to the chief of the town of Talladega. Give him this bowl so he will recognize that the message you carry comes from me. This responsibility is great, and I trust you to do this well."

Blue Fox listened closely to the message and then took the bowl from his father's hands. He set out on the trail that ran along the Chattahoochee River. Before he had gone far, he saw some of his friends playing in the water.

"Blue Fox," they called, "come join us."

It was early in the day and there was plenty of time to deliver his message. Blue Fox went down by the water where his friends were floating boats they had made of sticks tied together. Blue Fox had no boat, but the bowl in his hands was shaped like a boat. He put the bowl in the water and it floated away from him toward

48

the deep part of the river. It turned in a circle four times, and then sank.

Blue Fox was frightened. He could not carry his message without the bowl. He knew that the river was dangerous. It was said that there were tie-snakes, bright-colored creatures that would wrap themselves about swimmers who went into the deepest waters. Still, he was more afraid of disappointing his father. He swam to the place where the bowl had sunk.

"Blue Fox," his friends called, "be careful. The river is deep and the current is fast."

But Blue Fox did not listen. He dived down and he did not come up again. His friends waited for him until the sun was high overhead.

"Our friend has drowned," they said, and they went sadly back to Koweta town to tell the people of Blue Fox's death.

However, Blue Fox was not dead. As soon as he dived beneath the surface, many tie-snakes wrapped around him and carried the boy down to the very bottom of the river. When they set him free, he saw that he was in a cave.

"Climb up the s-stairs-s," the tie-snakes said.

Blue Fox looked at the stairs in front of him and saw they were made of living snakes all wrapped together. They were many colors: blue, yellow, red, white, and green. At the top of the stairs was a platform made of even more snakes. And on top of that platform sat a great tie-snake. Blue Fox knew immediately that the great snake must be the chief.

The chief of the tie-snakes wore a feathered headpiece and was black all over except for its throat, which was white. It had a hooked beak like a hawk's and its eyes glowed red as hot coals. Horns of brilliant blue and yellow grew from its head. Next to the great snake was the message bowl given to Blue Fox by his father.

Blue Fox tried to climb the steps, but as he lifted his foot, the steps moved and he stopped. It seemed to him that if he placed his foot upon the stairs, the snakes would tangle themselves about him and he would be crushed to death. He tried a second time. The stairs moved again, and he hesitated. He tried a third time and again pulled back as the stairs moved beneath him. Then he reminded himself of his responsibility. He had failed his father once, but he would not do it again. He placed his foot on the stairs and step-by-step climbed up to the place where the Chief of the Tie-Snakes sat.

"Welcome to my lodge. S-s-sit beside me," said the Tie-Snake Chief. The seat was made of living snakes, too. As Blue Fox approached, the eyes of those snakes followed him. It seemed that if he sat down, he would surely be killed. Blue Fox tried three times to sit. Then on the fourth try, he thought of the trust his father had placed in him. Only if he sat by the great snake would he have a chance to retrieve the message bowl he had been entrusted to carry. Blue Fox took a deep breath and sat down beside the great snake.

Then the chief pointed with its head toward a corner of the cave. "That feather is yours-s-s," said the Tie-Snake Chief.

Blue Fox went over to the tall feather. It was a heron plume like the ones on the great snake's headpiece. It seemed that there was so much power in the feather, it would burn him if he tried to touch it. But he reminded himself again of his responsibility. Three times he tried to grasp the feather, and three times its power was too great for his hand. On the fourth try, he said to himself, "I must be a man." Then he reached out and grasped the heron feather.

"You see that ax?" said the Tie-Snake Chief, motioning with its head toward another corner of the cave. "That ax is yours-s-s."

Blue Fox walked over to the ax and reached for it. It moved away from his hands and he could feel its power. He wondered if he was strong enough to hold it. Each time he reached, as he felt that uncertainty, the ax lifted itself above his grasp. But on the fourth try, he said to himself, "I am no longer a child; I am tall enough to reach this ax. I am strong enough to hold it." Then he reached for the ax and took it in his hand.

"You can return to your father now," said the Tie-Snake Chief. "Three days-s have passed in the world beneath the s-sky. He will as-s-k you where you have been. Tell him only 'I know what I know,' but do not tell him what you have learned. Do not tell him about the powerful things-s you have been given.

"S-soon you will need my help. You have proven yourself to be a young man who knows-s the meaning of res-spons-s-sibility. S-s-so I will help you. When you need my help, place my feather on your head. Walk to the eas-st and bow three times toward the ris-sing s-s-sun. I will come to help you."

Then the tie-snakes wrapped themselves around Blue Fox and carried him up to the surface of the water. As he stood on the bank, the tie-snakes dived back underwater and came up again with his father's message bowl. Blue Fox carried it to the village of the Talladega, where he placed it in the hands of the chief and delivered his message.

"We heard that you had drowned," said the Talladega chief. "Stay and tell us where you have been."

"I cannot say," Blue Fox said. "I must return to my father." Then he ran back to his village. When he walked into his house, his father welcomed him with joy.

"My son," the chief of Koweta said, embracing Blue Fox, "I thought you had drowned. Where have you been?"

"I have been with the tie-snakes. Their chief has instructed me to tell you only that I know what I know. I cannot tell you more," Blue Fox said.

Blue Fox's father looked at him. He could see that his son was not the same as he had been before. He seemed taller and straighter. Blue Fox had been touched by some power beyond that of human beings. So the chief accepted the words of his son and asked no further questions.

It was clear to the people of Koweta town, too, that Blue Fox was no longer the boy he had been. He carried with him the plume and the ax that the Tie-Snake Chief had given him, but would tell no one what they meant. His only answer to their questions was always, "I know what I know."

One day Blue Fox's father spoke to him. "My son, our scouts have brought a message. Our enemies from the lands of the Cherokee are coming to attack our village. There are many of them, and I am afraid they will kill us. Can you use what you know to help us?"

Blue Fox placed the feather on his head and took the ax in his hand. He walked down to the river, faced the rising sun, and bowed three times. When he raised his head after bowing the third time, the Tie-Snake Chief stood before him.

"My father needs your help," Blue Fox said.

"Tell him not to fear," the Tie-Snake Chief said. "Your enemies-s will attack, but all will be well." Then he was gone.

Blue Fox returned to Koweta town. By midday, the people heard the sound of many enemies coming. Soon a large band of Cherokee warriors was in sight walking along the bank of the river, ready to attack the town. Blue Fox raised his ax. As he did so, thousands of tie-snakes came crawling out of the water. They wrapped themselves around the feet of the enemy warriors until all of the attacking Cherokees lay on the ground, tangled in the coils of the tie-snakes.

Blue Fox approached them. "You must promise never to attack us again."

For a moment the Cherokees hesitated. But as Blue Fox raised his ax, all of the tie-snakes began to hiss and tighten their coils.

"We agree," said the captured warriors.

Once again, Blue Fox raised his ax. The tie-snakes uncoiled themselves and crawled to the side of the river bank.

The freed enemies looked at the snakes waiting near their feet and vowed even more strongly that they would always be friends of the Koweta. The power of Blue Fox was too great.

So it was that the Koweta were saved from their enemies. In time, just as his father had hoped, Blue Fox himself was chosen to be chief of the Koweta. And throughout his lifetime, his people lived in peace because of Blue Fox's visit to the underwater lodge of the Tie-Snake Chief.

The Wisdom of the Willow Tree
Osage

What is the meaning of life? Why is it that people grow old and die? Although he was young, those questions troubled the mind of Little One. He asked the elders about them, but their answers did not satisfy him. At last he knew there was only one thing to do. He would have to seek the answers in his dreams.

Little One rose early in the morning and prayed to Wah-Kon-Tah for help. Then he walked away from the village, across the prairie and toward the hills. He took nothing with him, no food or water. He was looking for a place where none of his people would see him, a place where a vision could come to him.

Little One walked a long way. Each night he camped in a different place, hoping that it would be the right one to give him a dream that could answer his questions. But no such dream came to him.

At last he came to a hill that rose above the land like the breast of a turkey. A spring burst from the rocks near the base of a great elm tree. It was such a beautiful place that it seemed to be filled with the power of Wah-Kon-Tah. Little One sat down by the base of that elm tree and waited as the sun set. But though he slept, again no sign was given to him.

When he woke the next morning, he was weak with hunger. I must go back home, he thought. He was filled with despair, but his thoughts were of his parents. He had been gone a long time. Even though it was expected that a young man would seek guidance alone in this fashion, Little One knew they would be worried.

"If I do not return while I still have the strength to

walk," he said, "I will die here and my family may never find my body."

So Little One began to follow the small stream that was fed by the spring. It flowed out of the hills in the direction of his village, and he trusted it to lead him home. He walked and walked until he was not far from his village. But as he walked along that stream, he stumbled and fell among the roots of an old willow tree.

Little One clung to the roots of the willow tree. Although he tried to rise, his legs were too weak.

"Grandfather," he said to the willow tree, "it is not possible for me to go on."

Then the ancient willow spoke to him.

"Little One," it said, "all the Little Ones always cling to me for support as they walk along the great path of life. See the base of my trunk, which sends forth those roots that hold me firm in the earth. They are the sign of my old age. They are darkened and wrinkled with age, but they are still strong. Their strength comes from relying on the earth. When the Little Ones use me as a symbol, they will not fail to see old age as they travel along the path of life."

Those words gave strength to Little One's spirit. He stood again and began to walk. Soon his own village was in sight, and as he sat down to rest for a moment in the grass of the prairie, looking at his village, another vision came to him. He saw before him the figure of an old man. The old man was strangely familiar, even though Little One had never seen him before.

"Look upon me," the old man said. "What do you see?"

"I see an old man whose face is wrinkled with age," Little One said.

"Look upon me again," the old man said.

Then Little One looked, and as he looked, the lesson shown him by the willow tree filled his heart.

"I see an aged man in sacred clothing," Little One said. "The fluttering down of the eagle adorns his head. I see you, my grandfather. I see an aged man with the stem of the pipe between his lips. I see you, my grandfather. You are firm and rooted to the earth like the ancient willow. I see you standing among the days that are peaceful and beautiful. I see you, my grandfather. I see you standing as you will stand in your lodge, my grandfather."

The ancient man smiled. Little One had seen truly.

"My young brother," the old man said, "your mind is fixed upon the days that are peaceful and beautiful." And then he was gone.

Now Little One's heart was filled with peace, and as he walked into the village, his mind was troubled no longer with those questions about the meaning of life. For he knew that the old man he had seen was himself. The ancient man was Little One as he would be when he became an elder, filled with that great peace and wisdom which would give strength to all of the people. From that day on, Little One began to spend more time listening to the words his elders spoke, and of all the young men in the village, he was the happiest and the most content.

THE SOUTHWEST

The people of the Southwest live in one of the most varied and beautiful places on the continent. The dry desert areas and the high mountains and mesas of the lands of the Navajo, Pueblo, and Apache peoples contrast with the seacoast and the river valleys that are home to the Yuki.

The Apache lived in the harsh deserts of what is now Arizona, moving seasonally to follow game and living in wickiups—portable dwellings that they covered with brush. Self-reliance was stressed as part of an Apache boy's coming to manhood. The Navajo, before the introduction of sheepherding, were much like their Apache cousins. They moved from one part of their territory to another and lived either in isolated hogans made of logs or in small family communities.

Both the Navajo and Apache gained a reputation for fierceness because of their defense of their homelands against those who sought to enslave or remove them.

That warrior tradition can be seen in such stories as the Apache tale "The Owl-Man Giant and the Monster Elk" and the Navajo story "How the Hero Twins Found Their Father."

The Pueblo story "The Bear Boy" is one that conveys a dual message. In a culture where people rely on one another and children are to be cherished, the neglectful father has as much to learn as the boy who wishes to become a man. And animals are seen not as mindless beings, but as wise creatures that can offer much knowledge to human beings who pay attention. In fact, the bear as a nurturing mother is a concept found almost everywhere in Native American culture. The turns of this particular story are ones that have always delighted me since I was first told the tale many years ago.

In California, things were not as hard as in the deserts of the Southwest. There, the Native people found that the climate was so mild and many kinds of food so plentiful, there was time for the development of complex family and community relationships. That complexity shows in their stories and rituals, as in the Yuki tale of one boy's initiation, "The Ghost Society."

The Owl-Man Giant
and the Monster Elk
Apache

Long ago, White-Painted Woman and her brother, Slayer of Enemies, lived on the earth. There were many monsters in those days, and one of the worst was Owl-Man Giant. Whenever Slayer of Enemies went hunting and shot a deer with his bow and arrows, Owl-Man Giant would come and take that deer. Owl-Man Giant was taller than the trees. He was hungry and fierce, and he wore a coat made of four layers of flint so that arrows could not kill him. Owl-Man Giant would come to the wickiup of White-Painted Woman and Slayer of Enemies and order them to give him food or he would eat them. White-Painted Woman prayed each morning that someone would help them.

One day, as she prayed, the Sun, who is the Giver of Life, came to her. "You are a brave woman," the Sun said, "so I wish you to be my wife."

White-Painted Woman agreed, and the two were married. But the Sun was not able to stay with her. His work was to bring light to all of the world.

"I must leave you," he said. "but you will have a child. He will be called Child of Water. You must hide him from the monsters. They know that he will destroy them when he is old enough."

Soon, White-Painted Woman gave birth to a boy. She named him Child of Water and hid him inside the wickiup in a hole under a basket in the corner. As soon as she hid him, Owl-Man Giant came to the door.

"I smell a child in there," the giant said. "I am hungry. Give him to me."

"There is no child in here," White-Painted Woman

said. And though Owl-Man Giant sniffed and searched, he could not find Child of Water. And so he went away.

One after another, each of the other monsters came to the wickiup seeking to eat the child, but White-Painted Woman kept him hidden and they went away.

"My son," White-Painted Woman said, "someday when you are grown, you will be very powerful. Then you will rid us of these monsters."

The boy grew quickly. One day he went to White-Painted Woman. "Mother," he said, "I am ready now to kill the monsters. Make a bow and arrows for me."

"First you must learn to hunt deer with your uncle, Slayer of Enemies," White-Painted Woman said. She made him a small wooden bow and arrows from the long grass.

Child of Water took the bow and arrows and followed his uncle. Slayer of Enemies led him along the canyons to the places where the deer could be found.

"Stay close to me," Slayer of Enemies said. "There are many monsters here in the canyons. Not only does Owl-Man Giant live nearby, there is also the Monster Elk. It is even bigger than Owl-Man Giant, and it tramples people before it eats them."

Child of Water listened carefully to his uncle and did as he was told. Soon they were able to creep close enough to a deer, and Child of Water shot his arrow. It struck the deer and killed it. But before they could reach the deer, Owl-Man Giant was there.

"This meat is mine," the giant said.

"My arrow killed the deer, so it is mine," said Child of Water. "You can have it only if you beat me in a contest."

"I agree," said Owl-Man Giant. "But I will set the

terms of this contest. Each of us will shoot four arrows at the other. You may go first."

"No," said Child of Water, "since I challenged you, it is right that I should allow you to go first."

Then Owl-Man Giant stepped back and picked up his bow, which was made from a huge tree. His four arrows were great logs with sharpened points. As he drew back his bow, lightning flashed all around them and a turquoise stone appeared at the feet of Child of Water.

"Pick me up," the turquoise stone said to the young man. "I will be your shield."

Child of Water looked to his uncle. Slayer of Enemies motioned for his nephew to pick up the stone. Child of Water held the turquoise stone before him. Owl-Man Giant fired his first arrow straight at the young man, but before it reached him, it rose up and went over Child of Water's head. Owl-Man Giant fired his second arrow, but before it reached the young man, it fell short. His third arrow went to the left, his fourth arrow to the right.

"Now," Child of Water said, "it is my turn."

Owl-Man Giant looked around for a stone that would protect him. He picked up a huge gray rock. Child of Water's first arrow split the rock and then knocked off the first coat of flint on the giant's armor. Owl-Man Giant picked up a bigger rock. But Child of Water's second arrow split that rock also and knocked away the next layer. Owl-Man Giant looked about for another rock but could not find one before Child of Water shot his third arrow, which removed the third layer from the giant's armor. Then, quickly, Child of Water fired his fourth arrow. It pierced the last coat of the giant's armor, went to his heart, and killed him.

Slayer of Enemies and Child of Water went back to their wickiup and told White-Painted Woman all that had happened.

"I do not believe it," White-Painted Woman said. "How can it be?"

When Child of Water showed his mother the pieces of flint from the giant's armor, she danced and sang with happiness.

"My son has come of age," she sang. "Now he will kill all the monsters that have troubled us for so long."

But Child of Water was not yet ready to dance and rejoice.

"Mother," he said, "I must go and kill the Monster Elk. It has been killing and eating the People for a long time."

Then Child of Water took his bow and arrows and set out. It was easy to find the trail of the Monster Elk. It was so huge and its hooves were so sharp that it left tracks in the stone. Some of those tracks can still be found in the stones to this day. Child of Water's plan was simple. He would shoot the great elk with his arrows. But when he stopped to sit down, he noticed that he had stepped close to a gopher hole and filled its entrance with dirt.

"Grandmother," Child of Water said, speaking to the gopher as an elder, "forgive me for blocking the door to your house." He leaned over and cleaned the dirt from the entrance to the gopher hole. When he had finished, the gopher stuck her head out of the hole.

"Grandson," said the gopher, "you have shown me great respect by clearing the doorway of my house and speaking to me as your grandmother. So I wish to warn you about the one you are hunting. The hair of the Monster Elk is so thick that even your arrows will not pierce it."

"What can I do?" said Child of Water. "This monster is eating the People. It will not be possible for human beings to live if I do not kill it."

"I will help you," the gopher said. "I know where the Monster Elk sleeps."

The gopher tunneled under the earth until she was beneath the place where the Monster Elk slept. She dug her hole right up to the monster's side, and she gnawed the hair away from the skin above its heart. There were four layers of hair, and the gopher had to work hard to remove all of them, but finally she was done. Then she went back underground to the place where Child of Water waited.

"There is only one spot where you can kill the horned monster," she said. "Shoot for the place over its heart where I chewed away all the hair."

"Grandmother," Child of Water said, "when I have killed the monster, you can be the first one to touch its body. That honor should be yours."

Then Child of Water continued on the trail until he was near the place where the monster slept. As soon as he was close enough, he shouted. The Monster Elk woke and jumped to its feet. Its horns were tall as trees. When it saw Child of Water, it bellowed so loudly that the ground shook. Child of Water drew back his arrow and let go. The arrow went straight to its target and struck the Monster Elk in its heart. The monster fell dead.

As soon as it fell, the gopher ran up to touch it. The

blood of the horned monster made her face and her paws dark. They are still dark to this day to remind people how she helped Child of Water.

When Child of Water came home, he called to his mother, "I have killed the Monster Elk."

"I do not believe it," said White-Painted Woman. "How can that be?"

Child of Water showed her the skin of the Monster Elk, and she rejoiced.

"My son," she said, "you have destroyed the monsters that have made this world unsafe for the People. The People to come will always remember you."

To this day, just as White-Painted Woman said, the Apache People remember Child of Water's great deeds, which made it safe for human beings to live on the earth. In honor of those deeds, they even made a special dance, to be danced whenever the People have to go to war. In it, the men play the part of Child of Water, and the women take the part of White-Painted Woman. It is a dance which reminds the People that when they go to fight, it should only be to protect the People from those who would destroy them.

How the Hero Twins
Found Their Father
Dine (Navajo)

One day long ago, Changing Woman was feeling lonely. She left her hogan and began to walk around. At last she came to a small waterfall. It was peaceful there, and she fell asleep with the sound of its water. As she slept, she dreamed that someone was there with her. When she woke, she saw footprints that had been burned into the stone. Those prints led to her from the east and went away from her to the west. So she realized that Sun had chosen her to be his wife.

In time she gave birth to two boys. She called them Older Twin and Younger Twin. Soon, however, the monsters who roamed the world in those days began to come to her hogan.

The giant Yeitso came to the hogan and loomed over it like a wall of stone. His skin was all covered with scales of flint, and he was taller than the hills. "Whose tracks are those around your hogan?" Yeitso rumbled. "They look like the tracks made by children at play."

"No," Changing Woman said, "I made those tracks myself with my hands. Because I am so lonely, I like to pretend that I have visitors."

That satisfied the giant and he went on his way. But other monsters continued to come and ask if there were children to be eaten. Finally, to discourage them and to keep her twin boys safe, Changing Woman grew cactus around the hogan. To this day, there is still cactus all over the lands where the Dine live.

As the boys grew up, they asked their mother one question again and again: "Who is our father?"

But she would never answer.

One day, when the boys were out together hunting for deer, Older Twin saw a tiny hole in the ground. Smoke was rising from it.

"Brother," he said, "look."

Younger Twin leaned over and touched the hole. As soon as he did so, a voice came from within.

"Grandchildren," it said, "come inside." Then the hole grew larger, and the twins went down into it on a ladder of thread that reached to the bottom. There, at the bottom of the hole, was an old lady. It was Spider Woman. She was the oldest of any beings on the earth, and those who respected her called her Grandmother. The walls of her cave were covered with beautiful feathers from all of the birds.

"Where are you going, grandchildren?" Spider Woman said.

"We are out hunting," Older Twin said.

"We want to find our father," said Younger Twin. "There are many monsters in the world, and they are troubling everyone. If we find our father, he may be able to help us destroy them."

"Your father is Johonaa'ei, the Sun," Spider Woman said. "I will help you find him."

Then Spider Woman gave each of the boys an eagle feather. "Keep these feathers," she said. "They will protect you. Now you must travel very far. Your journey will be hard, but my messenger Wind will go with you and show the way. First you must pass through Loka'aa Adigishii, the Cutting Reeds. If you remember the prayers I will teach you, you will pass through safely. But if you do not, the Cutting Reeds will kill you."

"Grandmother," Older Twin said, "we will remember what you tell us."

Grandmother Spider told them about the other dangers they would face on their way to the house of their father, the Sun. They would come to Seit'aad, Moving Sand. If they forgot their prayers and did not follow the right path, the sands would shift beneath them and then bury them. They would have to cross Nahodits'o, Swallowing Wash. It looked like the dry bed of a stream, but when people entered it, waters would rush in and they would drown. They would have to pass through Tse' Aheeninidil, Narrow Canyon, whose walls close in on travelers and crush them. In every place, if they took the wrong path or forgot to speak the right words, they would perish.

The twins were not afraid. Wind showed them the way, and they set out on their journey. Before long they came to the place where the reeds were sharp as obsidian knives. All around them they could see the bare bones of those who had tried to pass through and were killed by the reeds. Older Twin spoke the words they had been taught to the Cutting Reeds. "Loka'aa Adigishii," he said, speaking the powerful name of the Cutting Reeds, "allow us to pass."

The reeds were pleased to hear their name spoken. They parted, and holding tight to the eagle feathers, the twins passed through.

On they traveled until they came to Moving Sand. Now Younger Twin spoke to the sands.

"Moving Sand," he said, "allow us to pass."

The sands stopped shifting and the boys passed through. Wind showed them the way as they traveled, and soon they came to Swallowing Wash. This time Older Twin spoke.

"Swallowing Wash," he said, "allow us to pass." Then

the waters of Swallowing Wash became quiet and the boys passed through, following Wind, who showed them the way.

All went well until they came to Narrow Canyon. As they walked the trail into the canyon, both of the boys became afraid. The canyon walls started to close in on them, and they could not remember the right words to speak. But Wind blew on the eagle feathers and lifted them up high into the air. An eagle circled about them as they rose into the sky. The boys held on to their feathers and, flying with the eagle, they were carried to safety.

At last they came to the ocean. There two huge Water Striders waited for them. The twins greeted the Water Striders as Grandmother Spider had taught them.

"Talkaa Dijidii," the boys said, speaking the powerful names of the Water Striders, "we ask you to help us get to our father."

"We will carry you," said the Water Striders.

Older Twin and Younger Twin climbed on the backs of the insects, which carried them across the wide ocean to the land of Sun.

When they reached the house of the Sun, their father was not there. He had gone to travel all around the world as he did each day. Only a beautiful woman sat in Sun's hogan. She was the wife of Sun.

"Who are you?" she asked.

"We have come to see our father, Sun," Older Twin said.

"I believe your words are true, but my husband will not believe you," Sun's wife said. "Others have come here seeking power and claiming to be his children. He will try to kill you." Then she looked around the hogan.

On the east wall was a white curtain of cloud. On the south wall was a blue curtain of cloud. On the west wall was a yellow curtain, and on the north wall a black curtain of cloud. She reached out and pulled down the white cloud. "I will hide you from him," she said. She wrapped the boys in the white cloud so they could not be seen.

When Sun came home that night, the ground shook beneath his feet.

"Who has entered my hogan?" he asked.

But his wife would not answer him.

Sun began to look. He shook out each of the curtains. When he shook the last one, the white cloud on the east, the boys fell out on the floor.

"Father," Older Twin said, "we have come for you. We need your help to destroy the earth's monsters."

Sun did not believe the boys were his children.

"I must test you," he said. "If you are my sons, these knives will not kill you." Then he picked up the boys and threw them against the flint blades on the eastern side of his hogan. But the two boys held tight to their eagle feathers and flew above the blades.

"If you are my children," Sun said, "you can sleep in the ocean without freezing." Then he put the boys in the cold water and left them. Wind called to his friend the beaver, who came and warmed the boys so they did not freeze. When Sun came for them, they were alive and well. But he still did not believe them.

"I will make a sweat bath for you," Sun said. He called to his daughter and asked her to prepare a sweat house. The daughter did as Sun said. However, she had watched the boys pass the tests Sun gave them. She believed that the boys were his children, and decided to help them. When she made the sweat house, she dug a small hole at the back and covered it with a sheet of darkness and white shells.

"This is no ordinary sweat house," she whispered to the boys. "The lodge will be so hot that you will be killed. Climb into the pit in the back. You will be safe there."

As soon as the stones for the sweat bath were red-hot, Sun placed the boys in the lodge and covered it. The boys climbed into the pit in the back.

"Are you hot?" Sun asked.

"No," both boys answered.

Four times he asked, and four times they said no. Then Sun began to pour water on the hot stones in the middle of the lodge. The whole sweat house filled with scalding-hot steam. It was so hot that no human being could survive.

Sun waited a time before he spoke again. "Are you hot now?" he asked.

"Yes," both boys answered, "but the heat is pleasant."

At last Sun began to suspect that the boys were his children. But he prepared one more test. He filled a pipe with tobacco so strong that it would kill a normal person.

"We will smoke together," Sun said.

The boys agreed. Four times the pipe was passed around, but the boys held on to their eagle feathers, and the tobacco did not harm them. Now Sun knew they were indeed his sons.

"My daughter," he said, "prepare a bath for my sons." Then Older Twin and Younger Twin were bathed four times, first in a basket made of white beads, then in a basket made of turquoise, next in a basket made of white shells, and last in a basket made of black obsidian. Finally they were given new clothing.

"My sons," Johonaa'ei, the Sun, said, "I will give you the things you need to destroy the monsters." He reached up and took down two bows and two quivers of arrows from above his door. "These arrows are powerful weapons. They are the lightning that strikes crooked and the lightning that strikes straight. If I give them to you, you will surely kill the monsters. But when you have succeeded, you must return these bows and arrows."

"Thank you, Father," the twins said as they accepted the weapons.

"I must now give you new names," Sun said. "You who are older, your name is Monster Slayer. You who are younger, your name is now Born of Water because it was near the waterfall that I met your mother."

Then Sun dressed them in armor made of flint and lowered the two boys down to earth on a bolt of lightning.

When they stepped off the bolt, they were on top of Tsoodzil, Mount Taylor. As they walked down the south side of the mountain, they came to a high wall of stones.

"Brother," said Born of Water, "let us try our weapons and see how strong they are."

"That is good," said Monster Slayer.

So they shot their arrows. The lightning that strikes straight and the lightning that strikes crooked shattered the cliff, making a big cleft in it.

"We will do well with these weapons," Born of Water said.

As they walked down the mountain, they heard a rumbling like the sound of an earthquake. It was the giant Yeitso, who had smelled their scent and was coming to look for them, walking in a great circle around the hills. First they saw the top of his head over the hills to the east; then they saw his head and shoulders over the hills to the south. The ground shook even harder; and they saw the whole upper half of his body over the hills to the west. Finally the giant stood before them, just on the other side of Blue Water Lake. He bent over and drank until the lake was almost empty.

Born of Water and Monster Slayer stood upon a bent rainbow, and their reflections showed in the remaining water of the lake.

"What are these handsome little things?" Yeitso growled. "Why have I not seen them before, and how shall I kill them?"

Wind came to the shoulders of the twins and whispered to them. "Throw his words back to him."

"What is this big thing and why have we never seen him before?" the twins said. "How shall we kill him?"

Yeitso roared and fired an arrow at the boys. The bent rainbow on which the boys stood straightened, and the arrow passed over their heads. Yeitso fired a second bolt and the rainbow arced again. This time the giant's arrow passed beneath their feet. The giant's third arrow went to their left, his fourth to their right.

Then Born of Water shot his arrow. The lightning that strikes crooked hit Yeitso and knocked him back. Monster Slayer shot his arrow, and the lightning that strikes straight knocked Yeitso down and killed him. His flint scales shattered from his body and scattered all over the land.

"That flint will be useful to our people in the future,"

Monster Slayer said. Then the two brothers cut off the giant's head to make sure he would not come back to life again. As soon as they did so, Yeitso's blood began to flow down the valley.

"If his blood goes far enough, Yeitso will return to life," Wind whispered to the brothers. Quickly Monster Slayer cut a line in the rock and stopped the flow. Yeitso's blood dried and it remains there to this day, though the newcomers call it beds of lava.

Monster Slayer and Born of Water went home to Changing Woman. She did not believe what she was told until they showed her Yeitso's broken arrows, which they had brought with them. Soon the two brothers set forth again to slay the other monsters. They killed the One Who Kicks People Off the Cliffs; they killed the Monster Bird, the Eyes That Slay, the Bear That Pursues, and the Rolling Rock. Then they made a huge storm sweep across the land in the place where the monsters hid. When the storm ended, a great canyon existed where the many terrible creatures had once been. Today it is called the Grand Canyon by the newcomers.

"Now," Monster Slayer said, "we have killed all of the monsters that threatened the People."

But Wind came and whispered in Monster Slayer's ear, "Four still remain to bring death and trouble to the People."

So Monster Slayer and Born of Water set out to finish the work they had begun. They traveled in the direction Wind told them to go, toward the north. At last they found a cavern and went inside. This was the place where they would find the last ones that would trouble the Dine.

"Here is one of them," Born of Water said, standing

over an old man who crouched in a corner with an empty bowl. "It is Dichin." And indeed it was so. The old man was Dichin, whose name means "Hunger."

"I will kill you," said Monster Slayer. "Then the People will never again feel the pain of hunger."

"Do not kill me," said the old man. "It is hunger that makes food enjoyable. Without hunger the People would have no reason to go out and hunt for their food."

"This is true," said Monster Slayer. "We will spare you."

"Here," cried Born of Water, indicating an old woman wrapped in a blanket. "Here is one to slay. This is Hakaz Estan, Cold Woman."

Monster Slayer lifted up his hand. "Then she must die. No longer will the People shiver from the cold."

"No," said Cold Woman, "I am needed. Without me, the springs will dry up. The land will be too hot and the People will not survive."

"You are right," Monster Slayer said. "We must spare you also."

"This one here," Born of Water cried. "This one here with the ragged clothing is Tgaei. Surely it is right that we should destroy Poverty."

But Tgaei spoke up as the others had. "Without me, old things will never wear out. It will not be well for the People in the days to come if there is no poverty. Old things must wear out for there to be new ones."

"Then we shall spare you as well," Monster Slayer said.

"Brother," said Born of Water, "this old, old woman leaning on her stick is Sa. Old Age must be killed so that the People will not have to grow old and die."

But Old Age held up her hand. "No," Sa said, "you

must not destroy me. Without old age, people will not appreciate their lives. Let there be old age so that new people will have space to come into the world."

Again Monster Slayer and Born of Water had to agree. And so it is that hunger and cold, poverty and old age remain with us to this day.

Then Monster Slayer and Born of Water returned to their father, the Sun. They gave back their borrowed weapons, for the twins had done their work. But they were told that if they needed those weapons once more to save the People from monsters, they would be welcome in the house of their father to receive his help.

So it happened long ago, but the People say that the Hero Twins still have their dwelling in the valley of the San Juan River. Sometimes, when Dine men go to war, they go to that valley to pray for help from the Hero Twins. And if those old monsters—or new ones—come to threaten the lives of the People, the Dine know that the Hero Twins will visit the house of their father again.

The Bear Boy
Pueblo

Long ago, in a Pueblo village, a boy named Kuo-Haya lived with his father. But his father did not treat him well. In his heart he still mourned the death of his wife, Kuo-Haya's mother, and did not enjoy doing things with his son. He did not teach his boy how to run. He did not show him how to wrestle. He was always too busy.

As a result, Kuo-Haya was a timid boy and walked about stooped over all of the time. When the other boys raced or wrestled, Kuo-Haya slipped away. He spent much of his time alone.

Time passed, and the boy reached the age when his father should have been helping him get ready for his initiation into manhood. Still Kuo-Haya's father paid no attention at all to his son.

One day Kuo-Haya was out walking far from the village, toward the cliffs where the bears lived. Now the people of the village always knew they must stay away from these cliffs, for the bear was a very powerful animal. It was said that if someone saw a bear's tracks and followed them, he might never come back. But Kuo-Haya had never been told about this. When he came upon the tracks of a bear, Kuo-Haya followed them along an arroyo, a small canyon cut by a winding stream, up into the mesas. The tracks led into a little box canyon below some caves. There, he came upon some bear cubs.

When they saw Kuo-Haya, the little bears ran away. But Kuo-Haya sat down and called to them in a friendly voice.

"I will not hurt you," he said to the bear cubs. "Come and play with me."

78

The bears walked back out of the bushes. Soon the boy and the bears were playing together. As they played, however, a shadow came over them. Kuo-Haya looked up and saw the mother bear standing above him.

"Where is Kuo-Haya?" the people asked his father.

"I do not know," the father said.

"Then you must find him!"

So the father and the other people of the pueblo began to search for the missing boy. They went through the canyons calling his name. But they found no sign of the boy there. Finally, when they reached the cliffs, the best trackers found his footsteps and the path of the bears. They followed the tracks along the arroyo and up into the mesas to the box canyon. In front of a cave, they saw the boy playing with the bear cubs as the mother bear watched them approvingly, nudging Kuo-Haya now and then to encourage him.

The trackers crept close, hoping to grab the boy and run. But as soon as the mother bear caught their scent, she growled and pushed her cubs and the boy back into the cave.

"The boy is with the bears," the trackers said when they returned to the village.

"What shall we do?" the people asked.

"It is the responsibility of the boy's father," said the medicine man. Then he called Kuo-Haya's father to him.

"You have not done well," said the medicine man. "You are the one who must guide your boy to manhood, but you have neglected him. Now the mother bear is caring for your boy as you should have done all along. She is teaching him to be strong as a young man must be strong. If you love your son, only you can get him back."

Every one of the medicine man's words went into the father's heart like an arrow. He began to realize that he had been blind to his son's needs because of his own sorrow.

"You are right," he said. "I will go and bring back my son."

Kuo-Haya's father went along the arroyo and climbed the cliffs. When came to the bears' cave, he found Kuo-Haya wrestling with the little bears. As the father watched, he saw that his son seemed more sure of himself than ever before.

"Kuo-Haya," he shouted. "Come to me."

The boy looked at him and then just walked into the cave. Although the father tried to follow, the big mother bear stood up on her hind legs and growled. She would not allow the father to come any closer.

So Kuo-Haya's father went back to his home. He was angry now. He began to gather together his weapons, and brought out his bow and his arrows and his lance. But the medicine man came to his lodge and showed him the bear claw that he wore around his neck.

"Those bears are my relatives!" the medicine man said. "You must not harm them. They are teaching your boy how we should care for each other, so you must not be cruel to them. You must get your son back with love, not violence."

Kuo-Haya's father prayed for guidance. He went outside and sat on the ground. As he sat there, a bee flew up to him, right by his face. Then it flew away. The father stood up. Now he knew what to do!

"Thank you, Little Brother," he said. He began to make his preparations. The medicine man watched what he was doing and smiled.

Kuo-Haya's father went to the place where the bees had their hives. He made a fire and put green branches on it so that it made smoke. Then he blew the smoke into the tree where the bees were. The bees soon went to sleep.

Carefully Kuo-Haya's father took out some honey from their hive. When he was done, he placed pollen and some small pieces of turquoise at the foot of the tree to thank the bees for their gift. The medicine man, who was watching all this, smiled again. Truly the father was beginning to learn.

Kuo-Haya's father traveled again to the cliffs where the bears lived. He hid behind a tree and saw how the mother bear treated Kuo-Haya and the cubs with love. He saw that Kuo-Haya was able to hold his own as he wrestled with the bears.

He came out from his hiding place, put the honey on the ground, and stepped back. "My friends," he said, "I have brought you something sweet."

The mother bear and her cubs came over and began to eat the honey. While they ate, Kuo-Haya's father went to the boy. He saw that his little boy was now a young man.

"Kuo-Haya," he said, putting his hands on his son's shoulders, "I have come to take you home. The bears have taught me a lesson. I shall treat you as a father should treat his son."

"I will go with you, Father," said the boy. "But I, too, have learned things from the bears. They have shown me how we must care for one another. I will come with you only if you promise you will always be friends with the bears."

The father promised, and that promise was kept. Not only was he friends with the bears, but he showed his boy the love a son deserves. And he taught him all the things a son should be taught.

Everyone in the village soon saw that Kuo-Haya, the bear boy, was no longer the timid little boy he had been. Because of what the bears had taught him, he was the best wrestler among the boys. With his father's help, Kuo-Haya quickly became the greatest runner of all. To this day, his story is told to remind all parents that they must always show as much love for their children as there is in the heart of a bear.

The Ghost Society
Yuki

It was not yet morning, but Walks Slow could not sleep. If he was right, as soon as the morning light arrived, the men would enter the *han* and take him. They would spend the day making him ready, and then in the evening they would go to the *iwl-han*, the dance house. There Walks Slow—if he was one of the boys chosen this time—would be initiated into the Hulk'ilal-woknam, the Ghost Society. To belong to the Ghost Society meant that a boy was no longer a little child. He was one who had been taught the things that were needed to become a man. Still, the thought of having to face the powerful beings who came to do that initiation, beings who looked something like the older men of his village but who were actually powerful ghost spirits, worried Walks Slow.

This will happen, he thought. It was the right time of year, the season known as the Moon When Acorns Get Ready to Drop. He had seen the signs that preparations were taking place for the ceremony, even though no one spoke openly about it. It had been three winters since the last Hulk'ilal-woknam. And there was one every fourth year. Walks Slow was sure he would be chosen. He was old enough. He had seen three handfuls of winters. He was one of the boys who was praised for his ability to do things that helped the people. He was strong, a good hunter, a good runner. After the Hulk'ilal-woknam, he would be even stronger, even better at running and hunting. Surely he would be chosen.

Walks Slow had been through the Taikomol initiation three winters ago. They had taken him with the other children to the dance house early in the morning, and he had sat straight without moving from dawn till the middle of the day, hearing the old man with his cocoon rattle and eagle feather tell them the stories of creation that all true Yuki must know. Shum-hohtme, "Big Ear," was the old man's name, and he was a powerful man. His tellings of the ancient tales made them come alive in the darkened dance house.

Walks Slow's mother and father were behind him throughout the whole initiation, ready to prop him up if he wavered from his cross-legged stance or fell back as children sometimes did. But he sat straight and listened, taking into his memory every word.

Although he had done well then, he was still worried. He lay near the back of the house with his head close to the center post of their *han*, looking up at the roof overhead, the interlaced poles that were well covered with bark. The light flickered from the firepit, and a few sparks rose up like new stars going into the sky. He could see the entrance tunnel into their house, the woven basket door still closed. Soon it would be pushed aside and the men would enter. His hands were trembling. Walks Slow tried to calm his mind by thinking of the story old Shum-hohtme had told of how it all began, how the world was made, how the Taikomol-woknam came to be.

Even Taikomol, "He Who Walks Alone," made mistakes. It was from the north that Taikomol came. There was only water, no land, and Taikomol made land upon it. He built the first *iwl-han* on that land. He made human beings from sticks. But he had done this too quickly. The land sank, and the dance house and the first people sank with it. Again Taikomol was alone, with nothing but water around him.

So Taikomol created another world. There was no sun yet and no daylight and Taikomol had made no game animals to eat. In the darkness, the people hunted and ate one another. Things did not go right in that world. Fire came into it and burned everything up, even the water.

At last Taikomol made one more world. This time he started from the north and then extended it to the southeast. He made the sun, and daylight shone on the land. The land was new, white, and clean. He walked to the south, and as he walked, he saw the land stretching farther than he could see. But the land was not yet finished. Taikomol made rivers flow and mountains rise up. Then he built another dance house. The world swayed like a log floating in the water. The ground was not firm beneath it. Taikomol made a great elk, a great deer, a great coyote. He placed them in the north of the new land, but the land continued to move.

"Lie down and hold this earth firm," he said. They did so, and the land stopped swaying. As long as they lie still, the land is firm, but whenever one of them forgets and stands up again, the earth shakes. To this day, when earthquakes come, the people say it is because those animals are not lying still.

Then Taikomol went into his dance house. He placed sticks on the floor. "You will wake up as human beings and have a feast," Taikomol said. Then he went outside and stood at the door of the dance house. He waited all night. When it was morning, the sound of many voices talking came from inside the dance house. At last the first human beings emerged.

That was how it began, Walks Slow thought, with the new day. It seemed as if he could see the faintest glimmer of light from around the edges of the basket door. Suddenly the basket was snatched away from the door, and men came into the house. They grabbed him by the arms and feet and threw him out the door. In the early light of the new day, Walks Slow could see a few other boys outside. The men guided them from one house to another and then led them out of the village to the next settlement. By the end of the day, they had gathered boys from the camps all around. The twenty-four boys had been led through the woods. And now, as evening came, they were placed in front of the new *iwl-han* that had been built for this special occasion.

Walks Slow sat close to the door of the new dance house. He had been one of the first boys taken that morning and he had eaten nothing all day, but he was not hungry. Excitement filled his stomach. He was waiting for the drum. He knew it would be coming, for a handful of days ago, he had found the place where the men were building that drum. He had smelled the smoke and followed it through the hills until he heard the singing and looked down through the bushes to the place where the men were hollowing out the log. *"Helegadadie hiye, helegadadie hiye"* came the drumbeat song.

Then, from the dusk to the north of the dance house, he heard it coming. As the men carried the log, now painted the black that showed it to be a true drum, they sang that song, *"Helegadadie hiye."* As they reached the entrance, they swung the end of the drum in through the wood hole and then swung it out. Again and again they swung the drum, until on the fourth sacred time they actually brought it into the dance house. Soon, Walks Slow could hear the sound of the men's feet dancing on the drum, and he knew it was in its place over the ditch in the back of the house.

As the drum became silent, figures came out of the darkness and picked up Walks Slow, carrying him toward the door. They swung him four times and then released him to be caught by other hands inside. He blinked his eyes as he was seated, but he could see nothing. He could sense people standing about him and knew they must be the Hulk'ilal, the Ghosts.

Walks Slow trembled at the thought of their presence, recalling how Taikomol had put together the first Hulk'ilal-woknam. He asked his friend and helper Coyote to arrange the first ceremony, but Coyote did it wrong. Instead of having people wear costumes and play the part of the ghosts, Coyote brought in real ghosts. As a result, all of the people watching the ceremony or taking part in it died. Taikomol had to make new people. This time he arranged the ceremony himself instead of letting Coyote do it.

Walks Slow felt people moving about him in the dark. Then everything was still. All of the boys were now in their places in the dance house. Suddenly the fire burst up in the center of the house as the drum began to sound and the singing of *"Helina heluli, helina heluli, helina heluli, helina heluli"* began. Soon another noise split the air—the sound of men shaking their throats with their fingers as they shouted:

YUWWUWUWUWUW

Walks Slow wanted to jump up and run, but he could not. The ghosts were all around him and the other boys. They looked much like certain older men he knew well. But they were painted black and white in broad horizontal stripes. Their hair was not like human hair—it was as thick and stringy as maple bark. Their heads were circled by a wreath of black oak and manzanita leaves, their faces puffed out as a man's face would be if he stuffed his cheeks with grass. Something like a long, springy twig grew from the center of each Hulk'ilal's face, bent from the nostrils to the lower lip.

A human voice came from near the drum, speaking to the ghosts. "Where do you come from? Why are you here, saying nothing?"

Then the leaders of the ghosts hopped forward, twisting their arms back and forth. "We have come to see how you do this. We were sent by the One above. We came to see this fire, this drum, and the other things you are doing. We will not be here long."

Food was brought out, and it was given to the boys as they sat. Some, like Walks Slow, tried to refuse the food, but an older man who Walks Slow recognized as his mother's brother bent low and said to him, "This is the last food you will have for four days. Eat it while you can."

The Hulk'ilal then began to dance on the drum. One after another, each ghost leaped on the drum four times.

"Heye," shouted each ghost as he jumped.

"Yoho, yoho," the men in the dance house answered back.

The fire was built up even more, and it grew hotter. Everyone's body and face were beaded with sweat. All through the night the Hulk'ilal danced, and Walks Slow found himself not knowing if he was awake or asleep. It was a dance that would bring the people plenty to eat in the years to come. There would be deer and acorns and all other foods. At times more older men came into the house, and the dance-house leader greeted them, shaking his cocoon rattle. One of the old men was the father of Walks Slow's father.

A dance began and the boys were made to join in, and Walks Slow's grandfather danced behind him, keeping him close to the fire as they circled it, so that he would sweat even more. The dance leader grabbed a burning log from the fire and went about the circle, blowing sparks from it onto the boys.

"Yu'u, yu'u," Walks Slow's grandfather whispered in his ear.

Some shrank back, but Walks Slow held out his arms, crying the courage sounds his grandfather had reminded him of, "Yu'u, yu'u," even as the sparks landed on his wrists and forearms.

So it went on through that night and into the next day. They danced and sweated and sat and listened to the words and songs inside the dance house. Soon, there was no longer any awareness of day or night, or of any world other than that inside the dance house.

At last it was noon on the fourth day. Walks Slow and the other boys lay back as they had been told, their eyes closed, holding their breath as if they were dead. They were about to be born again. Walks Slow felt himself being lifted up, carried, and swung back and forth again and again and again. Suddenly he went flying through the air. He felt as if he were floating, as Taikomol must have floated before there was earth on which to walk. Then hands and arms caught him, and he opened his eyes. His parents and his grandfather and his aunt and uncle were holding him. They had caught him, just as the other boys were now being caught by their relatives as they were thrown out through the door of the dance house. The unfamiliar light of day made Walks Slow blink his eyes, but he laughed and his relatives laughed with him. He had been thrown out into manhood.

THE NORTHWEST

+

The stories that represent rite-of-passage experiences from the northwestern part of the American continent include tales from the buffalo-hunting peoples of the plains, the Cheyenne and Lakota, who maintained a chivalric code of honor in their lives as hunters and warriors; the people of the northern Pacific coast, where the lives and the stories of the people always focused on the sea; and the people of the northern coast of Alaska, where one of the most unforgiving climates in the world has bred a people who have learned every way to find the edge that will ensure their survival.

There are some elements in the stories from the plains that will be familiar by now. There is the vision quest in "The Light-haired Boy," the true story of a strange Lakota boy who wished to help his people by gaining power through fasting. In the Cheyenne tale "Star Boy," there is a mythic hero who has inherited power from his father, a sky-being, and uses it to kill the monsters that threaten his human relatives.

93

*The two stories from the far Northwest and the far-
thest north have some different events in them. In the
Tlingit tale "Salmon Boy," the hero not only goes down
to an underwater world, as the chief's son does in the
Creek story of the tie-snakes, but he is actually trans-
formed into a salmon himself. This story teaches
respect for the fish that are the source of life for his people, and it also makes clear how close the worlds of
humans and nonhumans are in the eyes of the Tlingit.*

*The true story "Tommy's Whale" was told to me
seven years ago in Alaska by the man who was that
boy (though his name has been changed in my telling).
It may require some further introduction, especially
since it is about the hunting of a great member of an
endangered species. As I hope this story makes clear,
the Inupiaq have great respect and even love for the
whale. As the Inupiaq poet Fred Bigjim puts it, "Bowhead whale, you give us our culture."*

*At one time, the bowhead whale was almost wiped
out, but it was not the Inupiaq who did that killing.
They never took more than they needed to live. Now
the number of bowhead has increased significantly.
Thousands of whales again swim beneath the ice of the
Bering Sea.*

*A few years ago, it was agreed by the International
Whaling Congress, in close consultation with the
Inupiaq Whaling Association, that the Inupiaq could
hunt the bowhead whale again, but only under the
strictest of controls. Each of a few villages is allowed to
strike no more than three whales each year. As my
friend who allowed me to tell his story said, "Even
now, though we hunt the great whale, we do so with
respect. We love the whale, and in return for our love it
gives itself to us."*

The Light-haired Boy
Lakota

It was the year 1841 and the time of the Moon of Falling Leaves. There, in the heart of the Paha Sapa, the sacred Black Hills, a boy was born. His father was Tashunka Witco, a holy man of the Oglala, one of the bands of the Lakota Nation. His mother was a member of the Brule Nation. Because this boy's hair was sandy brown, lighter, thinner, and curlier than any other Lakota boy's, he was soon given the nickname Curly.

As the seasons passed, the light-haired boy named Curly grew, but he did not grow as quickly as the other boys his age. He was strong and wiry, but he would never be tall. His hair and skin remained lighter than those of the other boys. They were so light that some of the Wasichu, those pale new people who liked to take the best of everything, sometimes thought he was one of them, a white boy who had been taken captive and adopted.

By the time Curly reached his thirteenth year, no one questioned that he was a real Lakota. He had killed a buffalo from horseback with his bow and arrows. He had been the first to ride a wild horse caught by his father. In fact, since he had ridden and been given that horse, his father and his father's best friend, a warrior named High Backbone, had a different name for the boy. They called him His Horse On Sight. But Curly was still the name spoken most often in camp.

Around the time Curly first learned to ride the wild horse, a meeting was held that would change the lives of many Lakota forever. It was August of 1854, in the Moon of Wild Plums. There was trouble between the Wasichu and the Lakota. A cow belonging to a settler had wandered into a Lakota camp circle. When it ran into his teepee, a man named High Forehead shot that cow. Then he butchered it and shared it with the people. After all, the promised government food rations were long overdue. It was only fair they should eat a cow that had volunteered itself in this way.

The matter should have been easy to solve, for though they joked about it, the Lakota were ready to pay for the cow. But that was not enough for the young warrior chief at the fort. He demanded of the Minneconjou band that Conquering Bear, one of the twenty-four chiefs of the Lakota Nation, meet with the white soldiers who were coming to the chief's village. And Conquering Bear must have High Forehead ready—to be handed over for punishment.

Conquering Bear agreed to the meeting. When the soldiers arrived at the Minneconjou village, not far from the Oglala camp where Curly lived, they were heavily armed. They were led by Lieutenant John H. Gratton. "Give me a handful of men and three cannons," Gratton had once said, "and I'll defeat the whole Sioux nation." Seeing this man at the head of the soldiers worried Conquering Bear even more, for they had brought the big guns carried in wagons. He had asked that no wagon guns be brought. Without wagon guns, they might be able to parley peacefully. Gratton, however, was spoiling for a fight. He ordered his thirty troopers to aim their carbines and the cannons at the lodge of Conquering Bear, where the chief stood with his other chiefs about him.

To make matters even worse, the Wasichu's interpreter, Wyuse, was known to be a man who spoke the truth only when it would benefit him.

"Minneconjou," Wyuse said, "you are dogs. You are cowards, men afraid to fight."

Then Lieutenant Gratton began to speak. His words were angry. It was possible that Wyuse interpreted them truthfully to Conquering Bear. But Conquering Bear's words were twisted like aspen leaves in the wind.

"We will give you five good horses for that one cow," Conquering Bear said in Lakota.

"The chief will not give you anything," Wyuse said in English.

"We do not wish to fight. We only want peace," Conquering Bear pleaded in Lakota.

"The chief says you are all afraid to shoot," Wyuse said in English, sneering.

As Wyuse spoke those words, Gratton barked an order. The thirty troopers fired a salvo. The men must have been nervous, for most of them failed to hit anything. But Conquering Bear's brother, who stood beside the chief, was struck in the chest by a bullet. Blood came from his mouth and he fell to the ground.

Some of the Lakota began to run. Conquering Bear stood his ground and held up his empty hands.

"Do not fight," he shouted to his people. "Now that the Wasichu have shot a good man, they will go away."

Even as Conquering Bear spoke, Gratton ordered another volley. The soldiers fired again, and three bullets struck Conquering Bear. He fell beside his brother. It seemed as if the Wasichu soldiers meant to wipe out the whole village. High Forehead grabbed a rifle and fired. His bullet hit and killed Lieutenant Gratton. Then the Lakota began to fight in earnest. Spotted Tail, another Lakota chief and the brother of Curly's mother, had been waiting with a group of his own men in a nearby ravine, in case of trouble. At the sound of the shots, they came running. Arrows rained down on the thirty soldiers. When it was over, all of the Wasichu were wiped out. So, too, was Wyuse, whose crooked words had made the trouble worse. His Lakota brother-in-law pierced the interpreter's ears with a lance. "Now," he said, "your ears are open. Next time they will not be closed when we speak to you."

That day, Curly was in the Minneconjou camp. From the other side, where he and a group of boys had been told to wait, he heard the shots and came running. The battle was over by the time he arrived. He helped other Lakota men and boys to overturn the wagon guns, pile brush over them, and set them on fire. Then he helped the Minneconjou break camp, and rode back to his own Oglala camp to help his own people do the same. They would move far away from the fort, for more trouble would surely follow this. Curly had learned a lesson that day. Never again would he trust the Wasichu soldiers. How could anyone trust people who would come into a peaceful camp and shoot a man in front of his own lodge?

For a few days it seemed as if the Lakota would have to go to war, but people on both sides spoke for peace. Among them was Conquering Bear, gravely wounded but not dead. The talk of war began to die down, and the soldiers at the fort did not retaliate. Gratton's actions had been provocative and war with the Lakota at this time was something no one wanted. The Oglala and Minneconjou moved even deeper into the Black Hills, away from the Laramie River and the fort. There, in the heart of the Paha Sapa, wrapped in his robes, Conquering Bear waited for his death.

High Backbone was one of Conquering Bear's most devoted warriors and kept vigil at the side of his dying chief. Because of High Backbone, Curly was allowed into the lodge of Conquering Bear. The sight of that gentle old man's drawn yellow face deeply affected the boy. He took his horse and rode away from the camp, knowing what he had to do. He rode along the bluffs above the river till he came to an eagle-catching pit dug into the soft earth. It was in such holes, concealed by branches placed on top with a freshly killed rabbit laid out for bait, that a man would wait for an eagle to land. Then he would grab the bird by its legs so that he could take some of its powerful feathers.

Curly tied his hobbling rope between the legs of his pinto so it would not wander far as it grazed at the bottom of the hill. The horse was close to a stream and could drink. He climbed the hill, stripped off all his clothes except for a breechclout, and stepped down into the uncovered pit. He sat back on the cold gravel, looked up at the sky, and prayed for a vision.

The first day passed and the night came. Curly did not leave the eagle-catching pit. He continued to pray for a vision, for strength to help his people in this hard time. The seasons to come would be even harder for the Lakota. He needed a vision to help them. But the second day passed, and the second night, and no vision came. Without food or water, Curly continued to cry for a vision.

"Wakan Tanka," he called, "Great Mystery, I am small and pitiful. I want to help my people."

It was a strange thing that the boy was doing on that hilltop. To fast and pray for a vision was not strange in itself. But *hanblecheyapi*, "crying for a vision," was one of the seven sacred rites of the Lakota people, and it was always supposed to be done in the right way. He had not done a purifying sweat to prepare himself. His elders had not prepared him for his vigil. His father had not taken him to the hilltop and showed him where to wait. But Curly continued with his strange vision quest, even after the dawn of the third day brought nothing to his eyes or ears. No spirit, no bird or animal, not even an insect came to him. All that he saw was the sky above and the earth and stones of the eagle-catching pit.

At last, late in the afternoon of that third day, Curly climbed out of the eagle-catching pit. After going so long without food or drink, he was barely able to stand. It seemed no vision would ever come to him, and he wondered if he was not worthy. He felt weak and sick as he made his way slowly down the hill to the place where his pinto grazed near a cottonwood tree. When he reached that tree, he could stand no longer. He slumped down against the tree and leaned his back against it.

And then the rider came. The rider came toward him on the back of Curly's own pinto, yet the horse and the man were floating in the air as they rode. They were more in the spirit world than in this world where Curly sat leaning against a tree. Suddenly the pinto changed. It became a bay horse, and then a spotted one. The man was closer now, and Curly saw that he wore blue leggings and had no paint on his face. His hair was long and brown, and a single feather hung from it. Behind one ear, a round stone was tied. A red-tailed hawk flew above the man's head. Then Curly heard words that were not spoken. They came to him from that warrior, telling him the day would come when he would dress that way. He would never wear a headdress or tie up his horse's tail, but he would be among the bravest of the brave.

The air became filled with the streaking of hail and bullets. Yet nothing touched that rider as he continued on. Storm clouds rolled above him and the thunder sounded, but the man continued to ride. Now there was a mark on the man's cheek like a lightning bolt, and spots on his chest like the marks of hail. Curly knew that he would paint himself that way one day when he rode to fight for his people. Then, as the man rode, there were people all around him, other Lakota. Some of them reached up to hold the rider back or pull him from his horse.

Curly felt hands on his shoulders, shaking him. He opened his eyes. His own father, Tashunka Witco, and his warrior uncle, High Backbone, were bending over him, concern in their faces. Curly looked past them and saw his pinto still grazing peacefully, hobbled as it had been before his vision began. No rider was on its back, but in the top of the bush next to the horse, a red-tailed hawk perched and called four times.

"Why are you here?" his father asked.

"It is not safe to ride off alone," High Backbone said. "There are raiding parties out, and the Wasichu may still make war on us."

"I came to seek a vision," Curly said. He wanted to tell the men what he had seen so they could help him better understand it. His father was a holy man and would surely know what it meant. But his father's face filled with anger.

"You were not prepared for *hanblecheyapi*," Tashunka Witco said. "How could you come out to fast without going first into the *inipi*, the sweat lodge? How can you expect a true vision without being guided by your elders?"

Curly looked over at High Backbone. He, too, was angry. They would not listen to him, so he said nothing. He did not speak of his vision. He let them carry him back to the camp, where he drank the soup given to him and then slept. When he woke, he still did not speak. He kept his vision in his heart but shared it with no one. Three winters passed, and his vision remained unshared.

Throughout those years, Tashunka Witco and High Backbone kept their eyes on the boy. They saw clearly that he had been changed for the better by whatever had come to him on that hill, but they did not ask him to tell of it.

Then, in the summer of 1857, during the Moon of Wild Plums, there was a great gathering of all the many camps of the Lakota Nation. Never before had Curly seen so many of his people together. All the Oglala, the Brule, the Minneconjou, the Sans Arc, the Blackfoot Lakota, the Two Kettles, and the Hunkpapa—the seven great camp circles—were there. They met in the valley below Bear Butte, in the heart of the Paha Sapa. Curly's heart was filled with love and pride for his people. And Tashunka Witco looked into his son's heart and saw that it was time for them to speak of what Curly had seen on his lonely vision quest.

The father and son rode off into the hills until they came to the valley near Rapid Creek on the eastern side of the Paha Sapa, where Curly had been born. Tashunka Witco constructed a sweat lodge and purified his son and himself. Then Curly began to talk. His father listened as he told of the powerful vision given to him.

Tashunka Witco was silent for a long time after his son finished. He looked into the fire and then spoke himself. "The man on that horse is the one you will become. You will dress and paint yourself as he did. You must always be first in fighting for our people, even though they will try to hold you back. And because of that vision, you must have a new name. I will give you my own name, and from now on, it will be yours to carry. From now on, you will be Tashunka Witco."

The young man whose name had been Curly listened to his father's words. He understood why his father had given him his name, for it fit his vision of a horse dancing through a storm. From that day on, he would be known by that name, and his name would come to stand for the bravest of all the Lakota. He would become a warrior who would never be touched by a bullet in battle, even though he was always in the front of every fight. He would be one of the principal leaders of the Lakota in the great battle at the Little Big Horn, where his people would defeat the Seventh Cavalry under George Armstrong Custer. In the days to come, his own Lakota people and all the world would know that name as it was said in English: Crazy Horse.

Star Boy
Cheyenne

Two young women walked out on the prairie one night to look up at the stars.

"I like that red star there," one of the young women said.

"I like that bright star better," said the other. "I wish it would come down to earth and marry me."

The next day, when they were gathering buffalo chips for the cooking fires, they saw a porcupine in the top of a small aspen tree.

"Let us try to shake it down to get some of its quills for decoration," the first young woman said.

"No," the second young woman said, "I will climb up and knock it off the limb with a stick." Then she began to climb. But the higher she climbed, the farther away the porcupine seemed to be. She looked down and saw that the tree was growing, carrying her far up into the sky. It took her right through the clouds, into the sky land. The young woman glanced around. The land was very much like the earth. The porcupine was no longer anywhere to be seen, but as she looked, she noticed someone walking toward her. It was an older man dressed in white skins. He took her by the hand.

"I heard you say you wished to marry me," he said. "Now you will be my wife. You will remain here in the sky land with me for the rest of your life."

For a while, the young woman lived happily with White Star. Her own name was now Star Woman, and the other people in the sky land treated her with respect because she was the wife of their chief. Although her husband was much older, he was always kind to her. After a year had passed, she gave birth to a baby boy. He was a strong and happy child like any other baby boy, except for one thing. On his forehead was a birthmark shaped like a star. Because he was the son of White Star, the sky chief, he was given the birthmark to show that he would have great power when he came of age. Star Woman was delighted with her child, but she began to think sadly of her own mother. My mother will never see her own grandson, she thought. Star Woman began to grow homesick for her people and wished she could return to them.

"I am going to dig roots," she said to White Star.

"That is good," he answered. "But do not try to dig up that plant with the red at its base. Its root is so deep that if it is dug out, it will make a hole in the sky."

Star Woman took her digging stick and went out looking for roots. As soon as she saw the plant with red at its base, she began to dig it up. It was not easy, but finally she was able to pull it out.

Where the plant had been, there was now a hole in the sky land. Far below she could see a circle of many lodges, and she knew it was the camp of her own people. She put the plant back into its hole and went to the lodge of White Star. There she began to make a rope by weaving together the grasses that grew in the sky land. Every day her rope was longer.

Finally she could wait no more. She was sure her rope was long enough. She took her baby and returned to that plant with the red at its base. She pulled it out and lowered her rope. It seemed as if it touched the earth below. She tied the end to a stick that she placed across the hole, and began to lower her baby and herself down.

When she got to the bottom, she was still high above the ground. Star Woman was not strong enough to climb back up. She held on for a time and then fell. It was a long fall. Star Woman was killed, but her baby survived.

The meadowlarks found the child and took pity on him. They fed him and kept him warm. As he grew stronger, he followed the birds as they flew, running beneath them. At last it came time for the birds to fly to the south land.

"I will come with you," said the boy.

"No," the meadowlarks said. "You've become tall and strong, but you are not a bird. Now you must return to your own people. You will learn how to become a man among them. Follow the river downstream and you will come to their camp circle."

Then the meadowlarks gave the boy a gift. They used some of their own feathers to make arrows and gave him a small, strong bow. "Use these to help your people and do not forget us," they told him.

The meadowlarks flew south, leaving Star Boy behind. Ever since then, the people have known that it is wrong to kill meadowlarks. And if you listen to their calls closely, you will hear that those birds know how to speak Cheyenne.

Star Boy began to follow the creek downstream. He walked a long way until he came to the edge of a big camp. There was a small teepee, and the door flap was open, so the boy walked in. An old woman was seated by the fire. She gestured for the boy to sit in the place of honor.

"Grandmother," Star Boy said, "I have come far to find you."

"Grandson," the old woman said, "I am glad you have come here. I would offer you water to drink, but there

is a great sucking monster that lives in the river. Whenever people go to get water, it sucks them in. Now all
of the people in the village have been swallowed, and I
am about to die of thirst."

"Grandmother," the boy said, "give me your bucket.
I will go and bring water back to you."

Star Boy walked down to the stream. He bent over
and began to dip the bucket into the water. As soon as
he did so, the sucking monster opened its big mouth
and drew him in. But Star Boy had brought his fire-
making kit and tinder with him. He made a fire, and by
its light he saw that all the people the monster had
swallowed were there in its belly with him.

Star Boy looked around until he saw a place in the
sucking monster's side that looked weak. He took out
his stone knife and cut a hole. As soon as he did this,
the monster floated up to the surface of the river and
died. Star Boy walked out of the sucking monster, and
all the people who had been inside followed him. He
bent down and filled his bucket, and then returned to
the camp with the rest of his people.

"Grandmother," he said, "here is your water to drink.
The sucking monster will bother the people no longer."

"Grandson," said the old woman, "you have done
well. It would be good to make a great fire and dance
about it to celebrate your brave deed. But we cannot get
more wood for a fire because of Great Owl. Great Owl
lives in the timber. Whenever people try to go into the
woods, it swoops down and carries them to its nest,
where it eats them."

"I will go and get wood," Star Boy said. He hung his
bow and arrows over his shoulder and went out into the
forest, where he began to chop wood. Before long, the

Great Owl heard the sound of Star Boy's stone ax. It floated down on silent wings, grabbed him in its talons, and began to fly to its nest. But Star Boy fitted an arrow to the string of his bow and shot it. The Great Owl fell to the earth, dead.

When Star Boy came back to the camp circle, he was carrying a great load of firewood.

"Grandmother," he said, "I have killed the Great Owl. No longer will it keep the people from getting firewood."

Then a great fire was built, and the camp crier went about calling everyone to rejoice. All the people came together and praised Star Boy. They danced and laughed and told stories until the sun rose the next day.

But when the sun rose, Star Boy was hungry.

"Grandmother," he said, "I am in need of food. Is there no buffalo meat?"

"Grandson," the old woman said, "there is no food in this camp. Whenever the men go out to hunt buffalo, the White Crow flies down and chases the animals far away. So we have no food to eat."

"Grandmother," said Star Boy, "let me take that old buffalo robe. I will see what I can do about the White Crow."

Then Star Boy put the buffalo robe over his shoulders and crept near the buffalo. He mingled in with the herd, and none of the buffalo paid any special attention to the old buffalo with the dirty hair that had just joined them. Before long, though, some young men came out from the Cheyenne village to hunt the buffalo. Before they could get close enough, a big white bird flew down to the buffalo herd.

"Run, run," White Crow cawed. "Run, run."

The buffalo herd began to run, and the old buffalo with the dirty hair ran with them. They left the Cheyenne hunters, who could not run as fast, far behind. But soon the old buffalo began to lag behind. Then it stumbled and fell.

White Crow flew down and began to circle over the old buffalo. "Are you dead, dead, dead?" White Crow cawed. "Are you dead, dead, dead?" The old buffalo did not move. Four times White Crow circled and called, but the buffalo did not move. At last White Crow settled down and landed on the old buffalo's back. He hopped up toward its head. As soon as he did so, Star Boy reached up from beneath the buffalo robe and grabbed White Crow by the legs. He tied White Crow's wings and carried him back to the camp.

"Here is your enemy," Star Boy said, and he handed White Crow over to the head of the Dog Soldiers, the society of men whose job it was to protect the people.

"I'll hang him over the smoke hole in my lodge until we decide what to do with him," the head of the Dog Soldiers said. Then he carried White Crow to his lodge and tied him up where the smoke was rising out of the lodge. White Crow hung there upside down, the smoke blackening his feathers. It was so hot in the smoke hole that White Crow grew smaller. The cords around him loosened and he became free. But he was White Crow no longer. Now he was black, as all crows are to this day. And he was no longer able to drive away the buffalo as he had when his feathers were white.

Once again the people could go out and hunt the buffalo with success. They were able to bring down enough buffalo to provide food for everyone in the village. As the people feasted, however, Star Boy's grandmother did not look happy.

"Grandmother," Star Boy asked, "what is wrong?"

"It is Winter Man," she said. "He is going to come soon. The snow will grow deep, and we will not be able to hunt the buffalo. Then he will begin to kill our people, especially the old ones such as me."

"Grandmother," Star Boy said, "come hunting with me. I will see what I can do about Winter Man."

Star Boy and his grandmother went out together to follow the buffalo. When they were far from the camp circle, Star Boy was able to kill a fat cow.

"Now we will cut this one up, Grandmother," he said. Yet as soon as the old woman began to butcher the buffalo cow, Winter Man walked over the hill. He was a giant taller than any man. He had a great club in his hand, and the north wind was at his back.

When he saw the old woman, he shouted, "Old woman, I am going to take that fat buffalo."

Star Boy's grandmother stood as if to run away, but Star Boy stopped her.

"I will stand by you, Grandmother," he said.

Winter Man came and stood over them. "This old woman has been walking around too long," he said. Winter Man lifted his club to strike, but Star Boy looked at him and his arm fell off. He lifted his other arm, and it dropped off, too. He tried to shout, and his head fell to the ground. Then, riding on the wind, Winter Man's wife came, grabbed the pieces of her husband, and carried him back over the hill.

Star Boy and his grandmother finished butchering the cow, wrapped the meat in its hide, made a travois, and dragged it back to camp. When they had shared the meat with the people, Star Boy turned again to his grandmother.

"Grandmother," he asked, "where does Winter Man live?"

"You must not go there," said the old woman. "He will have his great bow, and he will kill you because of what you did to him."

"Grandmother," Star Boy asked again, "where does Winter Man live?"

"You must not go there," the old woman repeated. "If Winter Man does not kill you, then his wife will kill you. She is as bad as her husband."

"Grandmother," Star Boy asked a third time, "where does Winter Man live?"

"You must not go there," the old woman said yet again. "All of his children are there and they are also dangerous."

The fourth time Star Boy asked the question, his grandmother finally told him.

"He lives in that cave alongside the river," she said.

Then Star Boy went straight to that cave. He walked inside, where Winter Man was being healed by his wife's medicine.

"Why are you here?" Winter Man roared, reaching for his great bow.

But Star Boy was faster than Winter Man. He grabbed the great bow before the giant was able to reach it.

"Uncle," Star Boy said, lifting up the bow, which was as big as a lodgepole pine log, "why is your bow so weak?" And he broke Winter Man's bow as easily as if it were a twig.

"Why are you in my lodge?" Winter Man roared again, reaching for his club.

Once more Star Boy was too quick. He grabbed the

club and raised it. "I have come to see how you are feeling, Uncle," he said. Then he struck Winter Man and killed him. He turned and struck Winter Man's wife, who was about to hit him with her own club. He killed almost all of Winter Man's children as they tried to kill him. And if he had killed all of those Winter Giants, winter would never again have come to the lands of the Cheyenne. But one small Winter Giant slipped out through a crack in the back of the cave. To this day he returns every year, and though he is not as fierce as his father, he is still dangerous, especially to the old people.

Then Star Boy returned to the village. Everyone celebrated his great victory. When several moons had passed, however, Star Boy looked up into the sky and knew that he could stay no longer. He went one last time to his grandmother's teepee.

"Grandmother," Star Boy said, "I have done all I can do among my mother's relatives. I have become a man here among the people of the Striped Arrows, but now I must go back to the land of my father."

With that, he began heading toward the east. He walked and walked until he was out of sight. And it is said that he traveled until he walked back up into the sky land. There, like his father, he became a star. Today he is the North Star and he can be seen every night, looking down from the center of the sky land on the camp circles of the Cheyenne.

Salmon Boy
Tlingit

One day, in the village of Sitka, a boy asked his mother for some food. It had been a long time since the salmon run, so all that she had was some dry salmon, which she gave to the boy.

"This is half-moldy," the boy said. "I will not eat half-moldy fish." He threw it on the ground and then stepped on it.

"The salmon *qwani* do not like to be treated that way," the mother said. "Whatever salmon we have to eat, we must be thankful for. We do not throw food away. If we throw food away, bad things may happen."

The boy, who was close to the time when he would be a young man, ignored her. He walked down to the water to try to catch some sea gulls with fish eggs on a small hook. He wrapped his line tightly around his wrist, baited his hook, and threw it into the water near the gulls.

Suddenly a huge sea gull, bigger than any bird he had ever seen before, grabbed his line and pulled him into the water before he could cut himself free. He tried to swim to shore, but the current was strong and the cold water deep. He called for help, but none of the people was near the water and no one heard him.

As he sank, a canoe full of strange-looking people came to him under the water. They were wearing clothing that shone as brightly as the scales of fish in the sun. It was the salmon *qwani*, the souls of the salmon that had died after swimming upstream to spawn. They pulled him into their canoe.

"Half-Moldy Boy," they said, laughing, "come with us."

Then the salmon people carried him out into the ocean to their village. The souls of the salmon looked just like people to the boy. Their village was much like his own village of Sitka. Although they called him Half-Moldy Boy, the salmon people treated him well.

"You must stay here with us now," they said. Then they showed him to a small house where he could stay. After a time, the boy became hungry. There was no food in the house. He looked all around the village.

"I am hungry. What can I eat?" Half-Moldy Boy finally said to one of the salmon people.

"You see those people there?" the salmon person said to him. "Just go over and say you want to wrestle with them. After a while, because you are strong, you will get a good hold and throw your opponent down. He will become food, which you may eat. Carry it away from the village and make a fire to cook it. But remember to burn all of the bones in that fire when you are through. Then come right back to our village and you will be surprised at what you see."

Half-Moldy Boy did as he was told. He wrestled with one of the young salmon men. When he threw that young man down, his opponent seemed to disappear. All that was left was a salmon at his feet. He carried it away, cooked it, and ate it. When he was done, Half-Moldy Boy was so eager to return to the village and see whatever it was that would surprise him that he hurriedly gathered the bones together and threw them quickly into the fire. When he arrived at the village, the young salmon man he had thrown down had already returned. But he was bent over, holding his back.

"Ah," the man said, "my backbone is hurting me."

Then Half-Moldy Boy realized he had been in such a hurry that he had not been careful enough. He quickly ran back to where he had eaten the salmon. There he discovered one tiny bone he had missed and threw it into the fire. When he returned again to the village, he found that the man's backache had disappeared.

As the days passed, Half-Moldy Boy was taught many things by the salmon people. He learned that there were songs and prayers of thanksgiving that a good fisherman must know. He tried to memorize them all so he would be able to take them back to his people. With those prayers and songs, his people would be able to do much better when they went fishing for salmon.

One day, many of the salmon people in the village started getting into their canoes.

"Where are you going?" Half-Moldy Boy asked.

"We are going to Copper River," one group said.

"We are going up to Dry Bay," said another.

So the salmon people spoke, referring to each stream where there would be a salmon run. Finally one group said, "We are going to the little river by Sitka."

"I will come with you," said Half-Moldy Boy. He climbed into a canoe and paddled with the others. All around him were many canoes filled with salmon returning home from the sea. The groups were going to the rivers where they had been born.

As the group he was with approached their river, the salmon people spoke with excitement about the coming battle.

"There will be forts in the river to stop us," they said, and the boy realized they were speaking about fish traps.

Every now and then, one of the salmon would tell another, "Ehaw! Stand up in the canoe and look around." And the boy would realize that meant jumping up out of the stream.

Soon they were in the river by Sitka. The boy saw his own mother there on the bank. He quickly stood up in the canoe, and his mother caught him as he leaped from the river.

"Look at the fine fish I have caught," she shouted to her husband. Then her husband noticed the copper necklace on the fish.

"What does this mean?" he asked, pointing to the necklace. "This is the necklace our son wore."

"Ehaw!" Salmon Boy's mother cried. "This is my son."

The two of them carried Salmon Boy home. They placed him on a shelf inside their house, surrounding him with eagle feathers. Then they called for the shaman. When the old man came in, he went straight to the shelf and examined Salmon Boy.

"It is my son," said the mother.

"I see who he is," the shaman said. "If you do as I say, he will be well." He heated oil in the fire and placed four drops on Salmon Boy as he lay there. With each drop, Salmon Boy grew a little larger. At last, the old shaman stepped back. "Cover him and leave him for the night," the old man said.

All through the night, the parents waited for dawn, praying that their son would be well. Every now and then, a noise would come from the shelf where Salmon Boy lay, but the parents did not uncover him.

When the dawn came, the parents removed the cover.

There was their son, fully human again. They lifted him up, and he embraced them.

"I have come back to help our people," Salmon Boy said.

From that day on, Salmon Boy always remembered the care one must take never to waste food and never, never to offend the souls of the salmon.

Tommy's Whale
Inupiaq

Tommy Anawrok had never gone out to hunt the bowhead before. But now he was about to climb into the umiak, the walrus-skin boat, with his uncle and his uncle's crew. His uncle had hunted whales for many years and was one of the most respected captains. Today they would go out into the Open Lead, where the ice had thawed and the whales would come to the surface.

Although Tommy was only thirteen and had never before gone on a whale hunt, he had known the bowhead whale all of his life. When he was six years old, a whale was brought up on the ice by his father's crew, and his father had taken the boy aside.

"My son," he said, "I want you to know the whale. We are going to leave this whale on the ice until you have touched every part of its body."

Tommy did as his father said. He spent a long time with the great whale there in the almost endless Arctic day of late May. He touched its flukes and its tail. He felt its mouth and the baleen through which it strained its food. He climbed onto the whale's back and walked up it, and found the place just where the head joined the body, where there was a small indentation. His father had told him to look for that place. In the old days, when a whale was struck badly and was suffering, the bravest and the best of the whalers would jump onto the whale's back and drive his harpoon down into that place. Then the whale's pain would be ended and it would die.

When he finished, the long day's light was dim and his father took him home and told him to sleep. That night he dreamed that he was a whale swimming beneath the ice, waiting to be called up by the people when they needed his help.

Tommy looked at the broad back of his uncle Tinuk, who sat in the front of the umiak. Tommy had great respect for his uncle. He found himself remembering words Uncle Tinuk had said to him long ago. "The greatest of all the sea animals is the bowhead whale. Long ago, when the Great Spirit had made all things, the Creator decided to make one more being, more beautiful and perfect than all the others. That being was the bowhead whale. Then the Creator saw that the Inupiaq people needed to hunt the whale to survive, and so the Creator gave them permission. But it was with the understanding that we would always show the whale respect.

"The Europeans have tried to separate us from the animals, from the sea," Uncle Tinuk had continued, "but every time they take an Inupiaq away from that life, they take a part of his spirit. Those animals are our lives in every way. We hunt them only because we need them to survive. That is why we use every part of an animal after we kill it, and we show it respect and thank its spirit."

Tommy had listened closely. He was only seven then, but he already knew that he would be a good hunter someday if he could be like his uncle. His mother had once told him a story about Uncle Tinuk.

"When your Uncle Tinuk was a boy," she had said, "he would go out hunting for seals with his gun. One time he went out with two of his older friends. Tinuk waited near one of the breathing holes for a seal to come out so that he could shoot it. His friends went around one of the pressure ridges on the ice, where the ice was pushed up twice as high as the roof of our house, to look for other breathing holes there. When they climbed up on top of the pressure ridge, they saw a polar bear only about fifty yards from Tinuk. It was down on its belly, crawling toward Tinuk the way a bear will when it is sneaking up on a seal. It was too far off for the other boys to shoot at it, and the wind was strong in their faces, so that they knew Tinuk would not hear their shouts. They could only watch.

"It seemed as if Tinuk did not see that bear. He kept sitting there, looking at the breathing hole in the ice. He did not move, and the bear got closer. Then, just when the bear was close enough to charge, Tinuk fired that little twenty-two. It hit the bear in its eye and killed it, like that. Tinuk had been waiting for the right time to shoot."

"It is true," Tommy's grandmother Belle had said from where she sat near the stove, sewing on a reindeer skin. "That is what my son did. He was like that boy in the story with the great eagle. He did not strike too soon."

Tommy knew that story about the great eagle. Grandma Belle told it often and Tommy never tired of it. Long ago, the whales began to vanish from the sea. The Inupiaq people lived near the foot of the big mountains by the sea. On top of one mountain a giant eagle lived, and down that mountainside a river ran. But instead of water, that river was full of whale oil. When the people saw oil in the river, they knew that the great eagle was catching all the whales and carrying them to the mountaintop.

The people knew that soon all the whales would be gone. So it was decided that someone must kill the great eagle. A boy whose name was Tinuk—the same name as Tommy's uncle—was the one who said he would go.

Tinuk took two spears and climbed the mountain and waited in a crevice. When the great eagle returned, carrying two whales in its talons, Tinuk did not move. Finally the eagle settled down. At just the right moment, Tinuk struck with his first spear. It wounded the eagle, which screamed and spread its wings to take flight. Then Tinuk stood so the angry eagle could see him. He waited as the eagle swooped toward him. Then he threw his spear, piercing its breast and killing it.

As Tommy joined the men in the umiak, he found himself remembering the story of the eagle. The importance of trusting himself was part of what it had taught him. But even more, the story had taught him that one could trust oneself only when prepared. The life of a hunter was dangerous. Anything might happen at any moment. Knowing what his body could do, knowing that his weapons were in good working order, knowing about the animals and the ice, the wind and the sea, were all necessary if he hoped to feed his family and return home safely. When a man went out in a small boat, he went only with men he knew would not foolishly put themselves or the others with them into a dangerous situation. That was the trust his uncle was showing him today.

The clouds hung low in the gray sky. The water of the Open Lead, the river of seawater that flowed through the ice at this time of year, was calm. The men's snowmobiles with their sleds attached to the back, burdened with ropes and the block and tackle to pull a whale up on the ice, shrank until they could no longer be seen.

"Keep watching to all sides," Uncle Tinuk said, and Tommy narrowed his eyes behind the dark lenses. Like his uncle, he wore sunglasses against the glare. In the old days, the Inupiaq had made their own "sunglasses," carved with a small slit in the center, which were strapped over the eyes. Two of the old men still had such goggles. But most of the best hunters now used modern sunglasses. He lifted his head up even higher to keep watch.

Fred Anawrok, his older cousin, chuckled from behind him. "Tommy," he said, his left hand steady on the handle of the outboard motor, "you look like that big eagle your grandma tells about in that story."

"There." Tommy's uncle spoke from the front of the umiak. The motor roared, and they turned hard to the starboard side. There were two whales ahead of them, swimming on the surface. As they came closer, Uncle Tinuk raised the gun to his shoulder, aiming for the spot that would kill the whale as quickly as possible. It was not right that any animal should suffer, even though it was necessary to hunt it.

Tommy held his breath, waiting for the shot. But his uncle kept waiting. Then, as the whale surged up, he fired. The blast of his shot rang in Tommy's ears. Just as he fired, however, the boat struck a wave and drifted away from the whale. They brought the boat close again. A second shot was fired. It, too, went wrong. The whale continued to swim, its blood flowing into the sea.

The long harpoons in the boat could be used now, but the strike would have to be clean and sure to kill the whale. Suddenly Tommy knew what he had to do. He stood and called to his uncle.

"Give me the harpoon," he said.

Uncle Tinuk and the others in the umiak looked at him. Everything was silent. It seemed as if even the sound of the outboard motor and the splashing of the whale as it swam were gone.

Uncle Tinuk took the harpoon and thrust it, point first, at Tommy. It was a gesture that might have made another person sit back down or flinch, but Tommy reached out his hand for the harpoon. He took the cold metal in his hand, and a look passed between him and his uncle. Uncle Tinuk understood that now was Tommy's time to try. Holding the harpoon across his body for balance, Tommy moved toward the starboard side of the umiak where the whale swam. He took a deep breath and jumped. All of the balance that hunters train for served him well. He landed on the whale's back and did not fall off, even though the water washed over his ankles and his knees. He made his way up the whale's back until he stood over the place he had touched when he was a small boy, that indentation where the whale's head joined its body. He lifted the harpoon.

Then, with all of his might, he struck down. The sharp harpoon plunged through the skin and fat and bone. The whale quivered once, the full length of its huge body, and then died.

Tommy felt hands grasping him, pulling him into the umiak. His uncle and his cousin were patting him on the back as the other men fastened the ropes to the bowhead to tow it onto the ice. But Tommy saw only the great whale, and he spoke the words he had learned long ago.

"Bowhead," he said, "thank you for giving us our lives."

AFTERWORD

I owe much to the elders who shared stories with me, but I could not have told the ones in this collection had it not been for my two sons, who helped me better realize what I had been taught as I tried to pass it on to them.

I listened to many voices as I put this book together. Some were the voices of teachers who had, in a physical sense, passed on. But I only needed to be silent for a moment to hear again the gentle and strong voice of my friend Swift Eagle, the Apache/Pueblo storyteller who once reminded me to listen to the voice of the leaves. In that same silence, I could also hear the clear, teaching words of Maurice Dennis, the Abenaki tradition-bearer whose Indian name, Mdawelasis, means "Little Loon." And there were others, so many I cannot list them all.

I tried, as I wrote, to keep in mind the meaning of the name given to me a decade ago by Clan Mother Dewasentah of the Onondaga Nation. That name, Gah-neh-goh-he-yoh, means "The Good Mind." To keep a good mind means that one must always try to speak with honesty and honor and keep one's thoughts away from selfishness and vanity, especially when speaking on a topic as important as the passage of a boy from childhood into young manhood.

With that in mind, it is important for me to say one more thing. All of these stories are wiser than I am. Their messages come from many generations, and if these tellings of mine have meaning for those who read them, it is only because I have succeeded to some small extent in being true to the original voices that spoke them.

There is such a wealth of traditions and so many hundreds of volumes devoted to the stories of different Native American nations that a truly representative bibliography would be far too long to include. Further, many books put together by non-Natives during the nineteenth and twentieth centuries have mistold Native stories. I strongly urge readers to turn to books written by Native people themselves. There is a new generation of Native American writers and storytellers whose work is both accurate and exciting. An excellent introduction to many of the central ideas of Native American life, including material on storytelling and rites of passage, is *The Sacred* by Peggy Beck, Anna Lee Walters, and Nia Francisco (Tsaile, Ariz.: Navajo Community College Press, 1977).

Some other books of interest are:

Erdoes, Richard, and Alfonso Ortiz, eds. *American Indian Myths and Legends*, New York: Pantheon Books, 1984.

Hilbert, Vi, trans. and ed. *Haboo: Native American Stories from Puget Sound*, Seattle: University of Washington Press, 1985.

Tehanetorens. *Tales of the Iroquois*, Rooseveltown, N.Y: Akwesasne Notes Press, 1976.

Zuni People. *The Zunis: Self-Portrayals*, Albuquerque: University of New Mexico Press, 1972.

About the Author

Joseph Bruchac is a storyteller and writer whose work often draws upon his Native American heritage. His stories and poems have appeared in more than four hundred anthologies, and he has written several books, including *Thirteen Moons on Turtle's Back* and the *Keepers of the Earth* series, coauthored with Michael Caduto. Mr. Bruchac is the recipient of the American Book Award for editing *Breaking Silence*, an anthology of Asian-American poetry; the Parents' Choice Award for *Gluskabe Stories*, a storytelling tape of traditional Abenaki tales; and the Hope S. Dean Memorial Award from the Foundation for Children's Books for developing a body of work that promotes an appreciation of children's literature. Mr. Bruchac lives in Greenfield, New York, with his wife, Carol, and their two sons, Jesse and Jim.